WALLS

Israel and Palestine

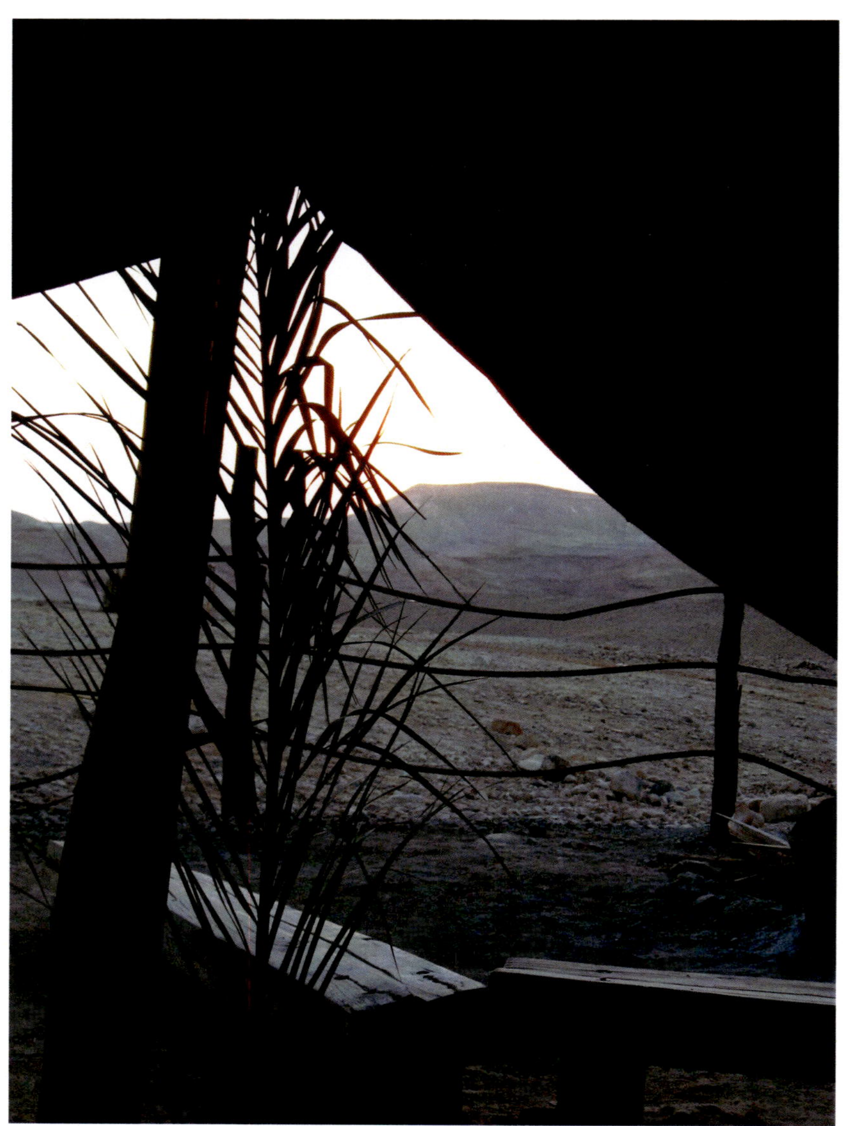

Negev Desert 2007

WALLS
Israel and Palestine

Photographs by
Henry Ralph Carse

Edited by Marcus Reichert

ZIGGURAT BOOKS
International

Henry Ralph Carse is a pilgrim, scholar and practical theologian who has lived in the Middle East for forty years. A graduate of Hebrew University (Jerusalem), The General Theological Seminary (New York) and the University of Kent at Canterbury, his Ph.D. thesis in theology is a post-modern study of pilgrim narratives. Dr. Carse is the Founder of Kids4Peace USA, a non-profit organization bringing together Israeli and Palestinian youngsters, with their American "peace-pals," for interfaith encounter and dialogue across the lines of prejudice and conflict. He now resides in Vermont.

For Danny,
who sees the inscape.

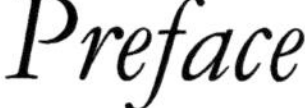

Preface

WALLS
Israel and Palestine

"In Jerusalem, within those ancient walls ...
the prophets are sharing the history of the holy."
                              – Mahmoud Darwish

"There's a wall between you and everyone else ...
and a wall that cuts deep within yourself."
                              – Yehonatan Geffen

The leading edge of a large incomplete concrete
barrier, advancing week by week through an arid
landscape, is blunt. Not in the sense of "my brother's
opinions are always refreshingly blunt," but rather as
in, "the victim was bludgeoned in her sleep with a
blunt implement."

The smooth presenting face of a finished wall,
however, is so sharp as to be sheer. Not like "sheer
coincidence;" more like "sheer force." A wall's surface,
like a layer of graphene one atom thick, is less yielding
than steel, defining as it does, in only two dimensions,
"here" from "there." Choose. No compromise is
possible.

Or so it seems. Actually, no one has ever built a wall that could entirely protect the innocent, punish the guilty, separate pure from impure, or thwart the human gaze.

Our fingertips seek nuance and the invisible crack of doubt, so they probe, caress and examine until they are roughened raw. Compelled by irony or yearning, by courage or desperation, by whim or terror, we mark our walls with graffiti shibboleths. Also, for good measure, we access them with gates and checkpoints, festoon them with searchlights and razor wire, and placard them with warnings, invitations, epithets, funeral notices, mottos, manifestos and snippets of gallows humor.

Our gaze assaults our walls until we are exhausted and heartbroken. Serving our time, we scratch every surface we can reach, hoping in vain to discover a breach to freedom, or at least a few rough millimeters of "in-between." Yet even a full-fledged window, blasted somehow, hypothetically, at great risk to both sides, into the concrete barrier between us, could never reveal to us the human face "over there." All we see is the framed fragment that we are barely prepared to countenance. In the end, our walls remain our mirrors.

In these few photographs from Israel and Palestine,
all I have been able to do is wipe my inexpert sleeve
briefly over this mirror's surface; the dust is only
disturbed, not removed. I reach the enclave of your
gaze, not with the wrecking ball of conviction, but
with a camera's doubtful lens. You may not need
anyone's blunt opinions or sharp insights. In refuge
or ghetto, detention camp or study hall, bomb shelter
or grave, you may need nothing, least of all these
reflected glimpses of our peripheral and internalized
barriers. Here, nonetheless, they are.

For the Palestinian poet Mahmoud Darwish, the walls
of Jerusalem are the thinnest of veils, revealing rather
than concealing the naked city's irresistible allure. For
the Israeli songwriter Yehonatan Geffen, countless
barriers stand in the Unholy Land, between Abraham
and his sons, between evil and innocence, between
friend and foe. Photographs, like poets, do not need
to explain; our inner eye will see – or fail to see – their
meaning.

Henry Ralph Carse

February 14, 2011
Eothen, Vermont

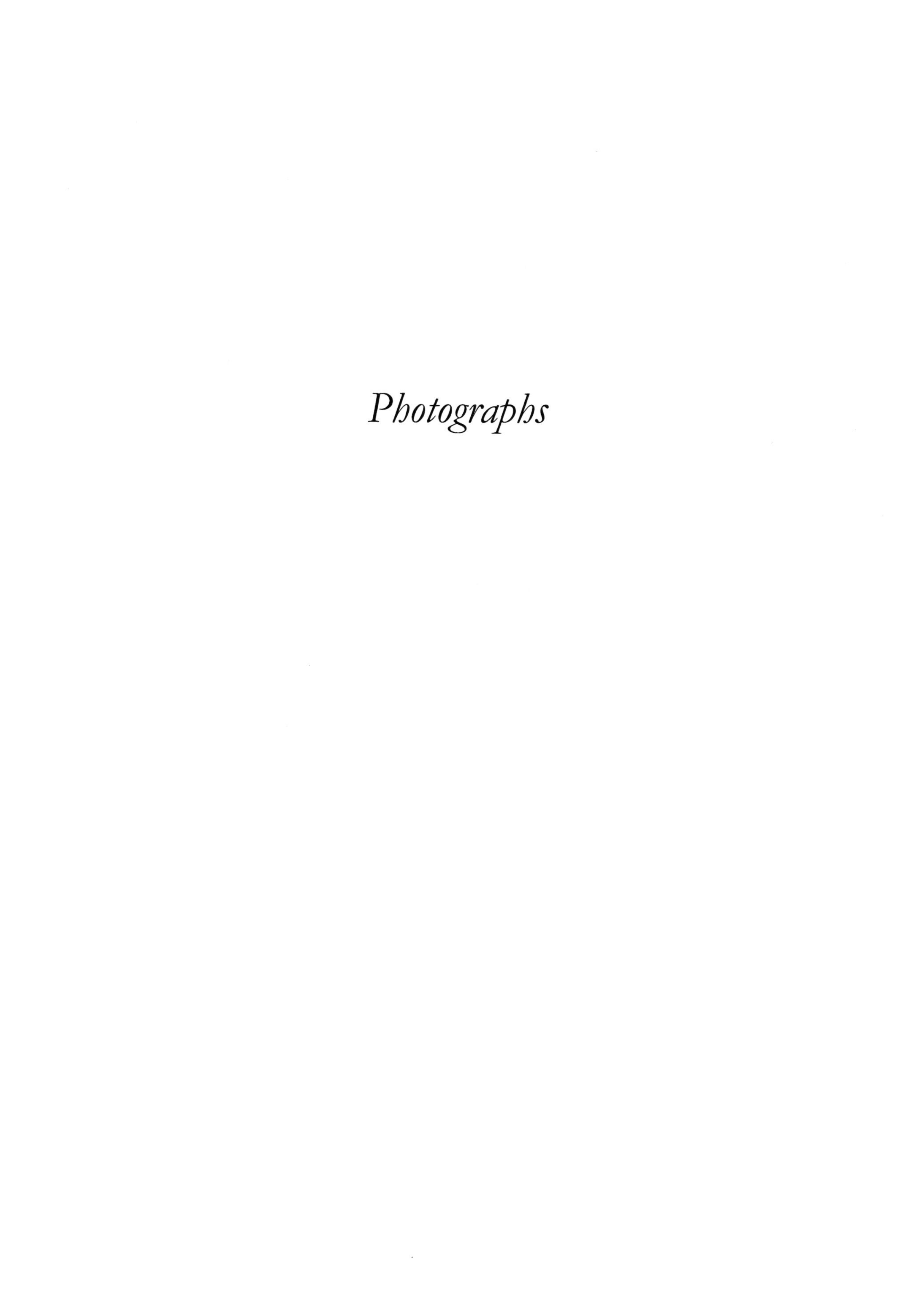

Photographs

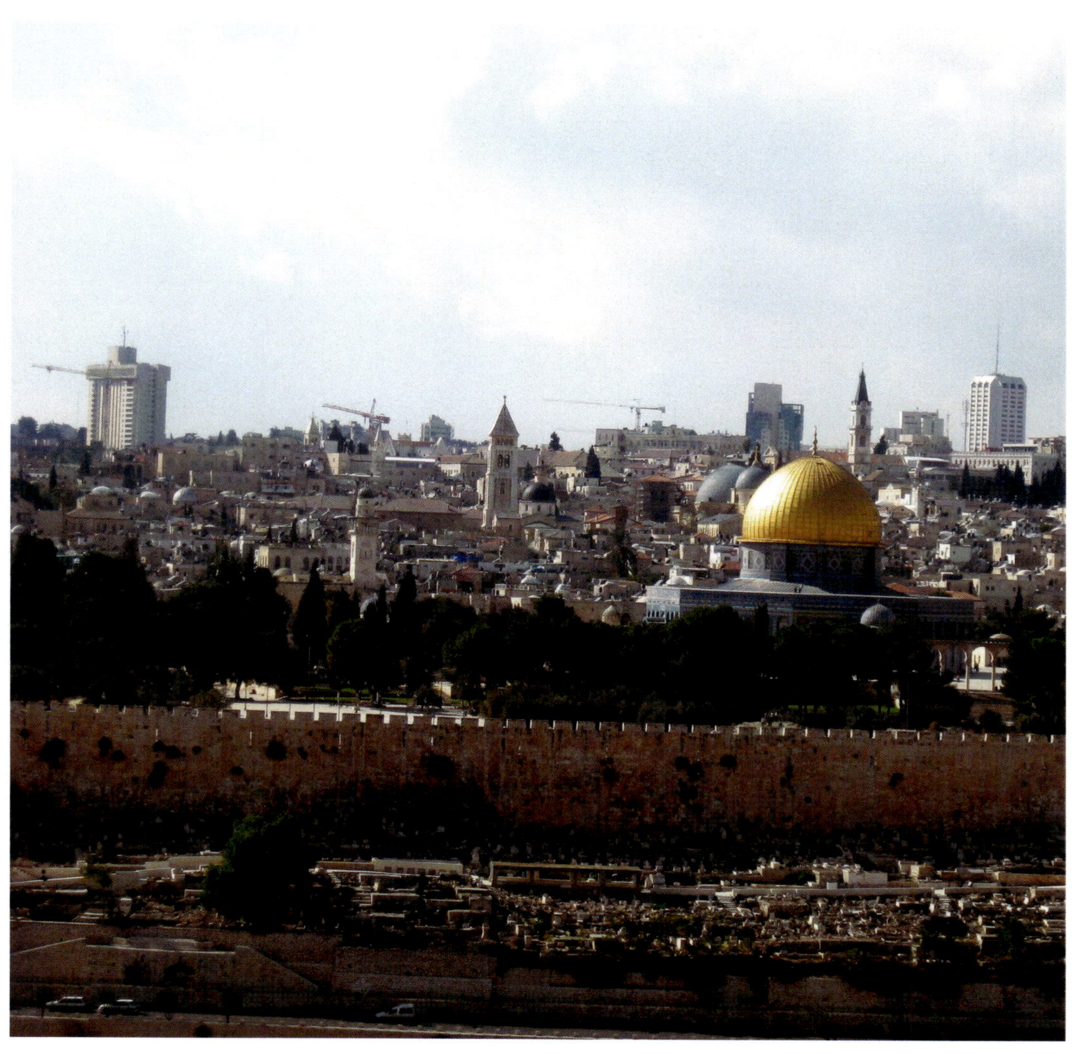

Old City, Jerusalem 2008

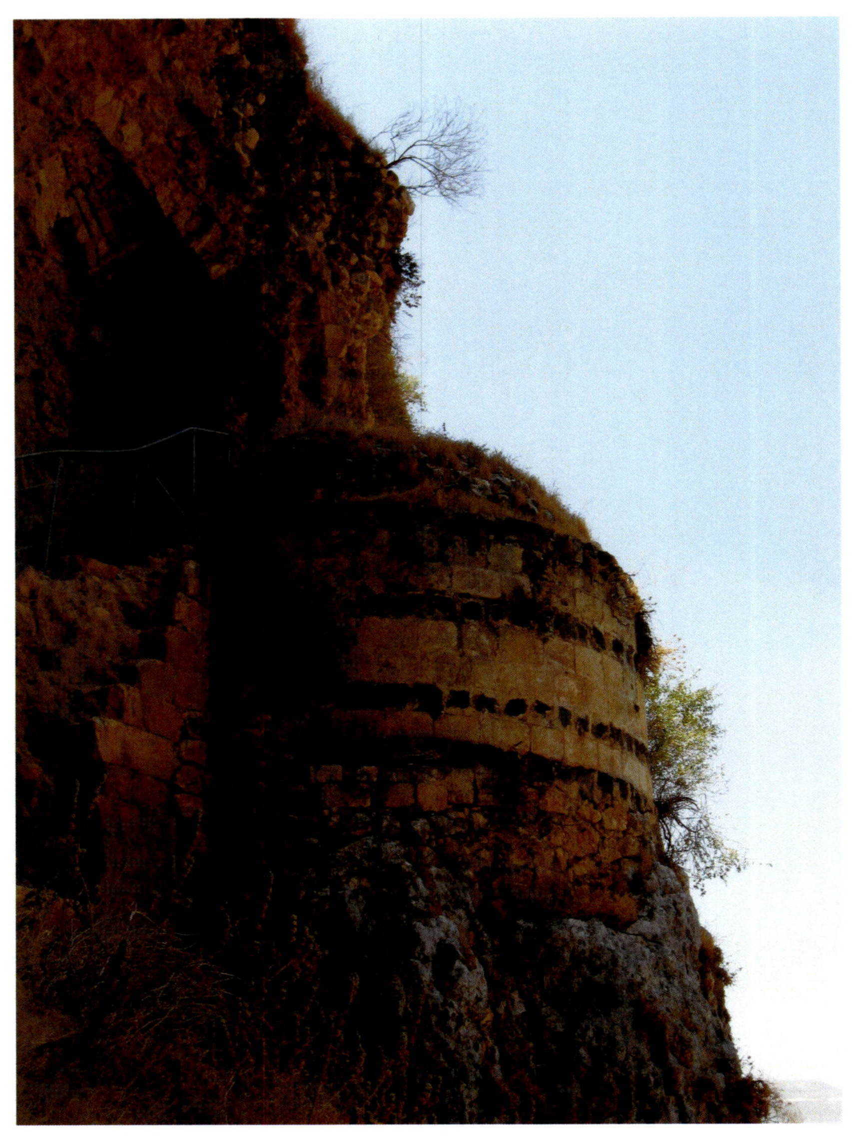

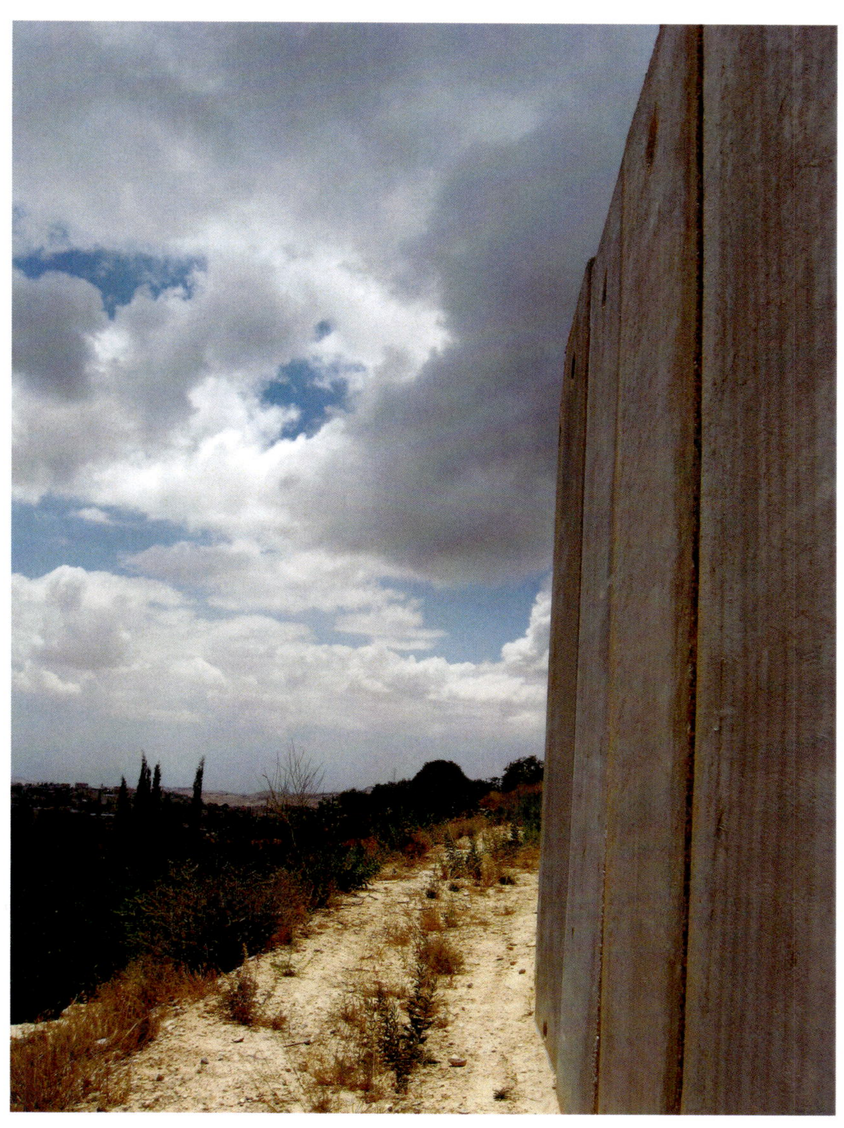

Separation Wall 2010

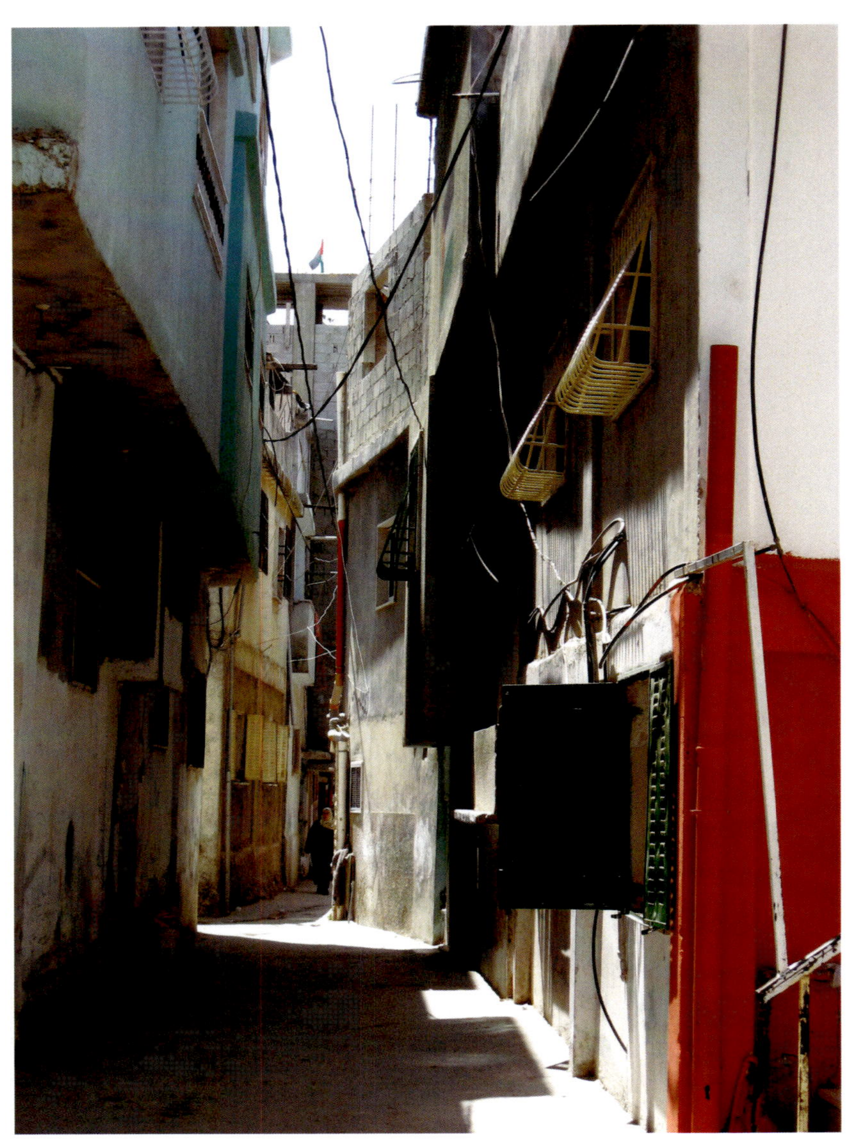

El Arroub 2010

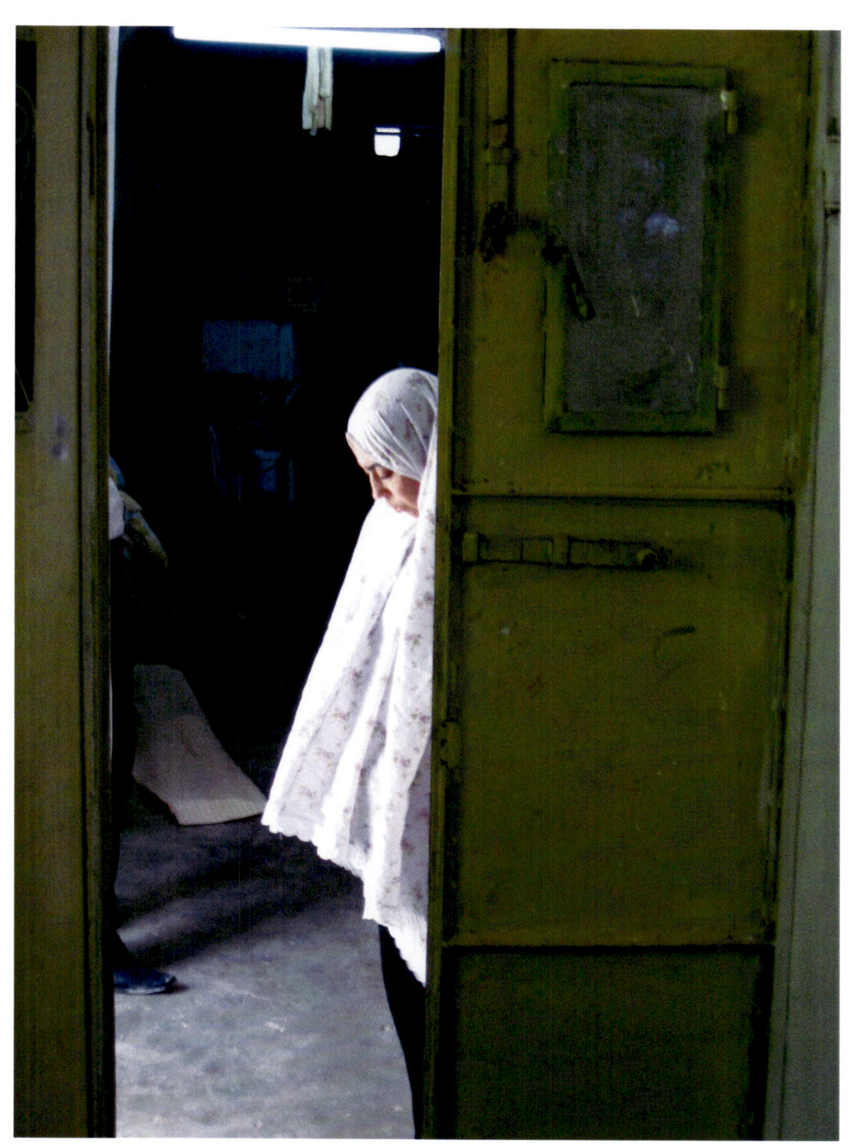

El Arroub 2010

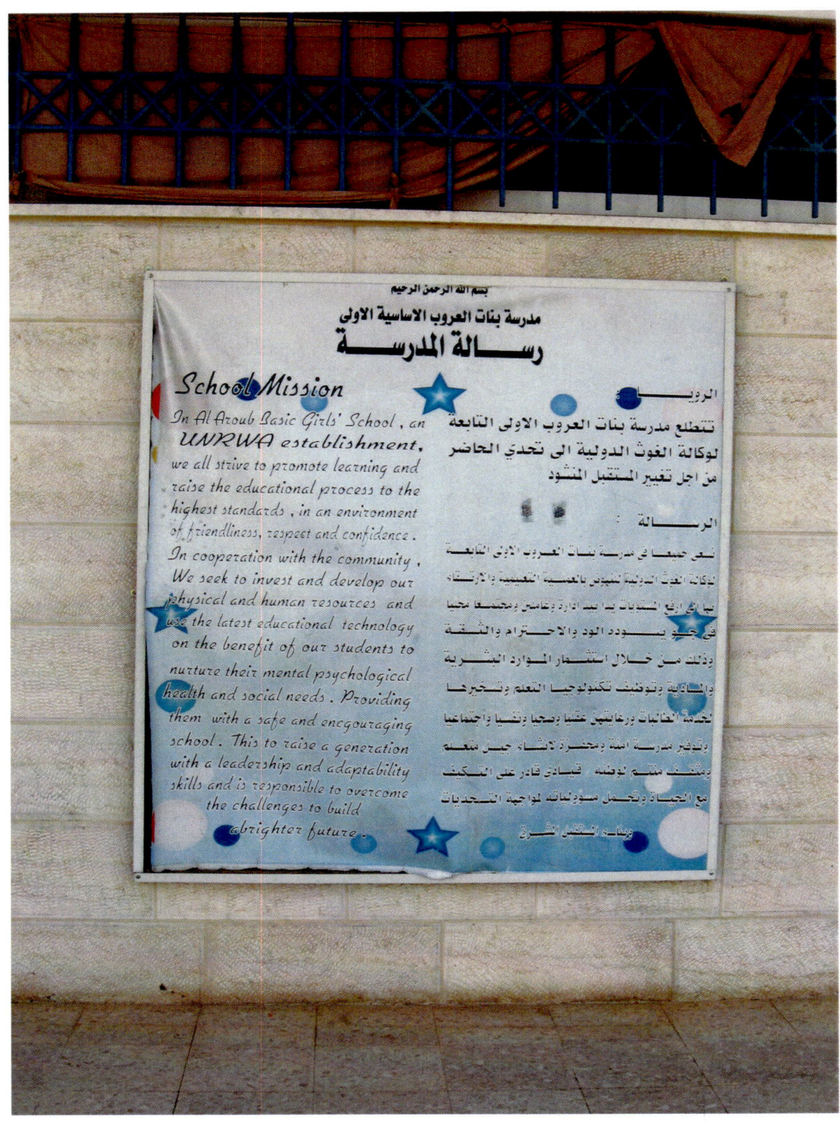

El Arroub 2010

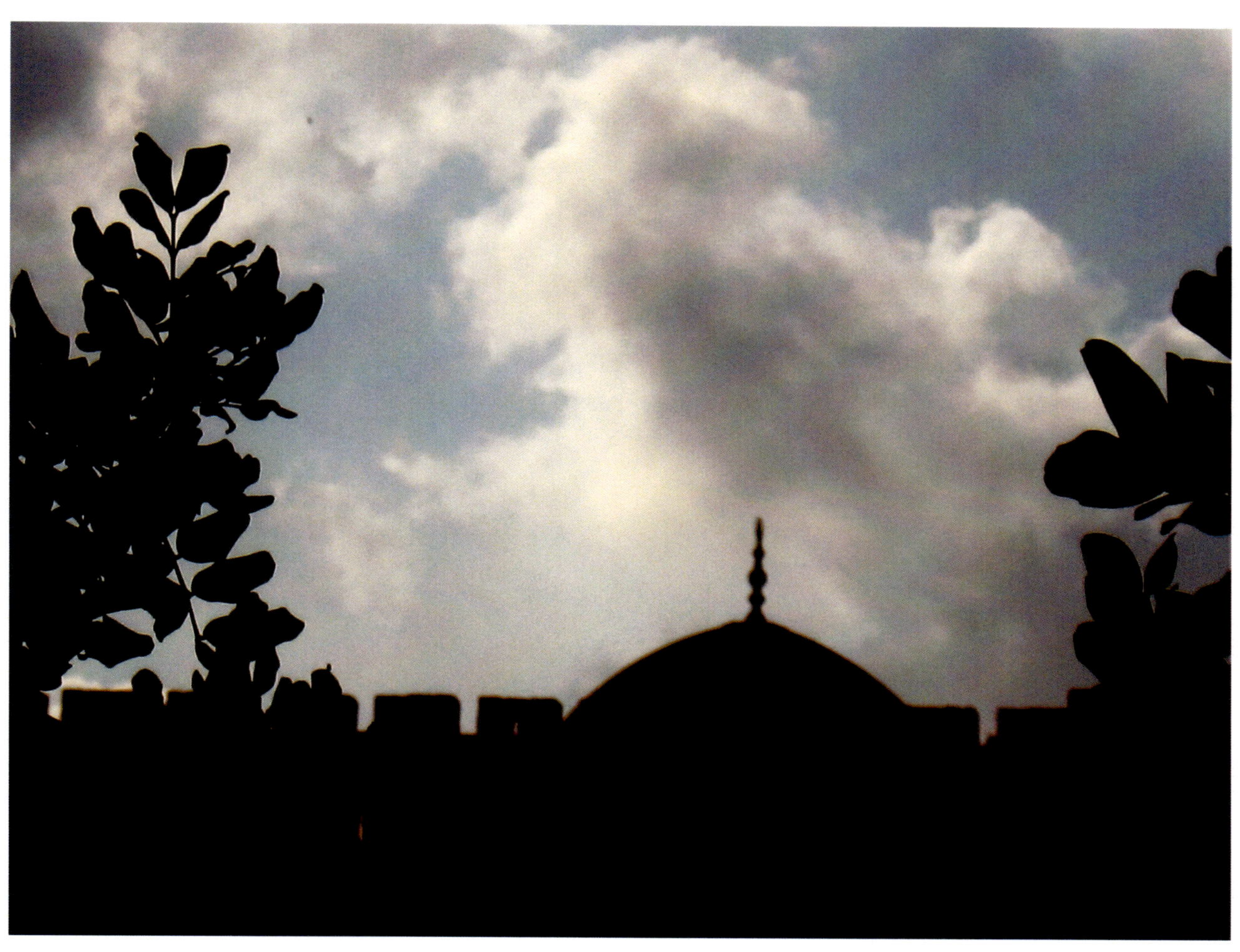

Old City, Jerusalem 2008

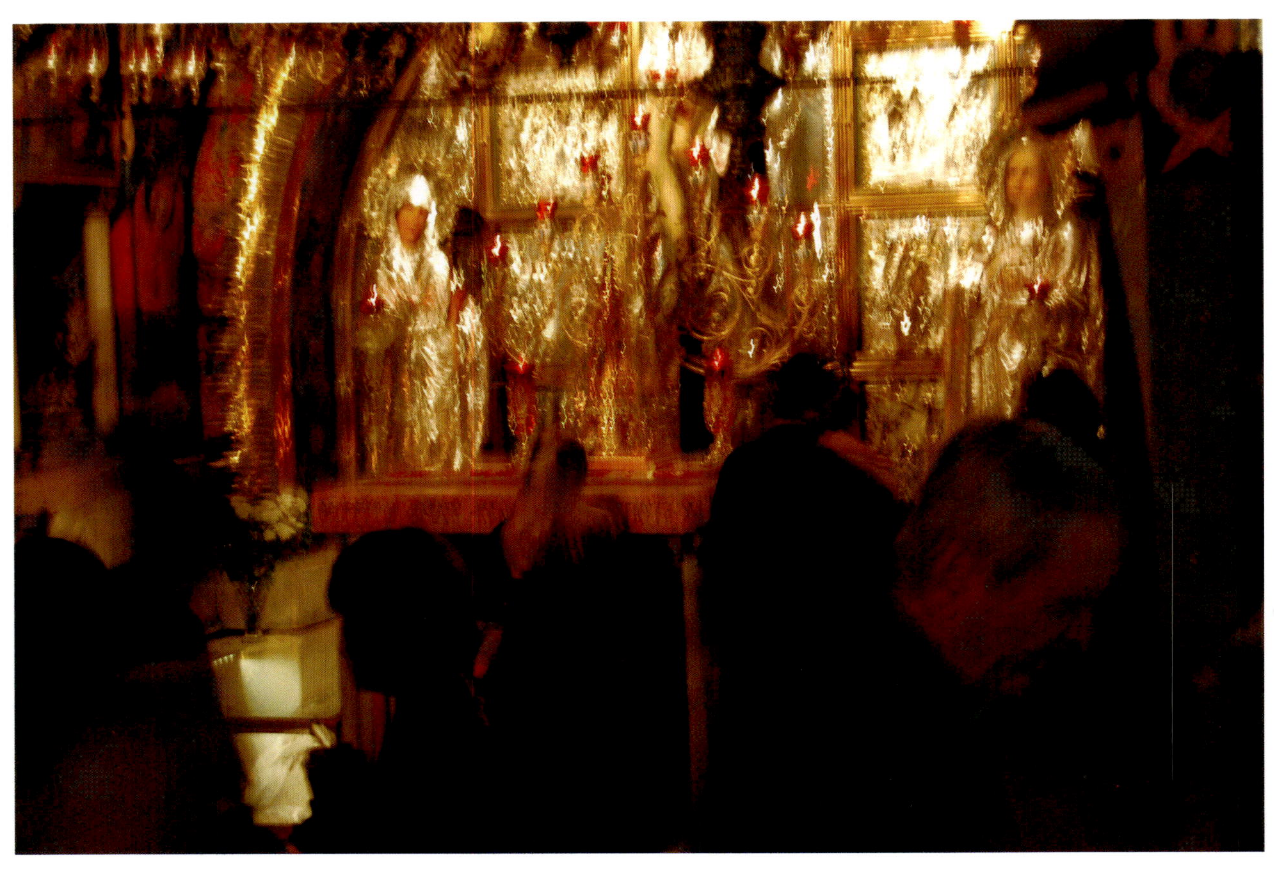

Golgotha 2009

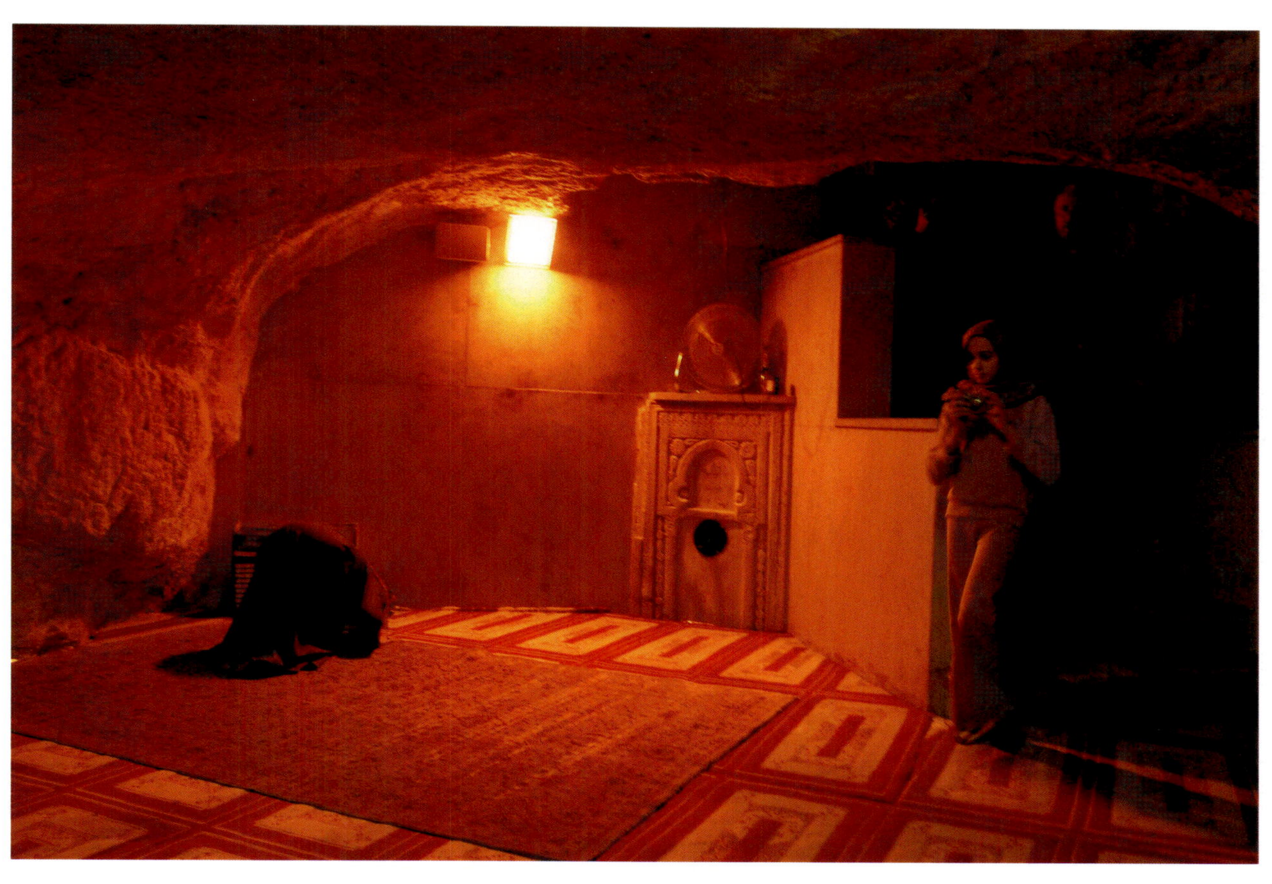

Dome of the Rock 2009

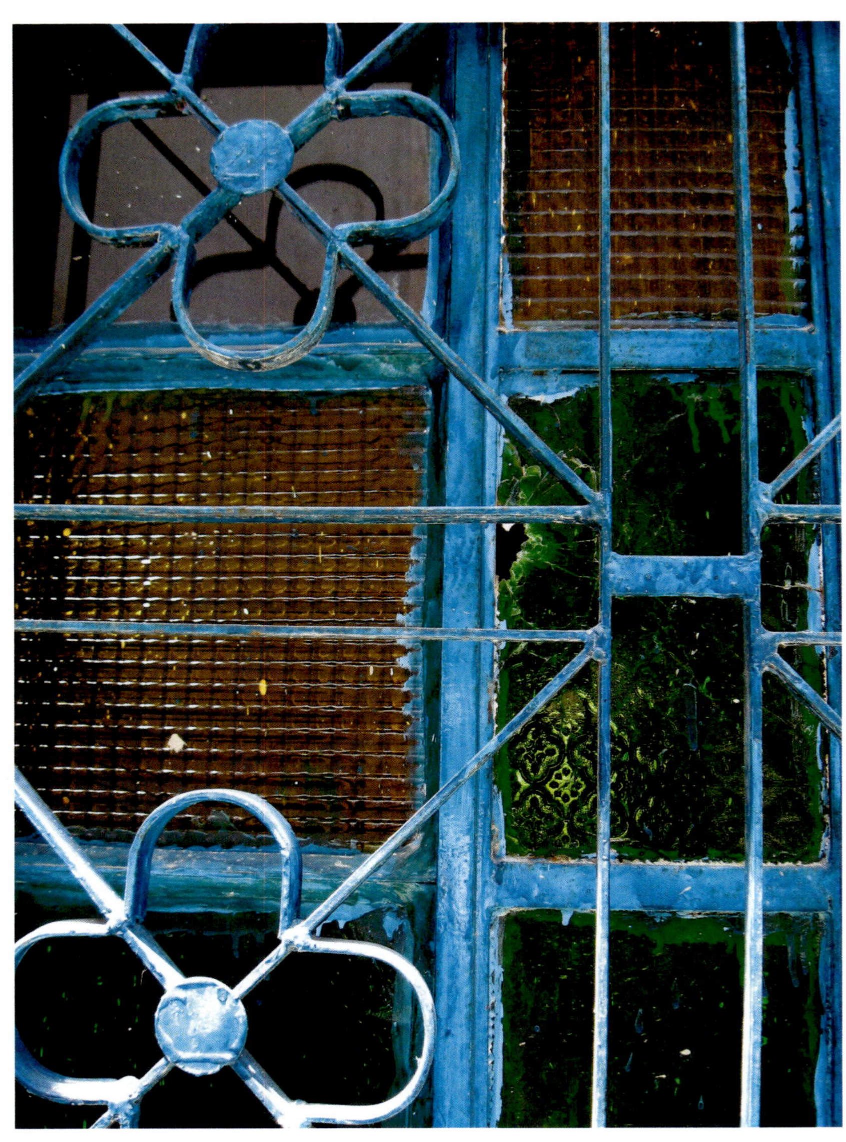

El Arroub 2010

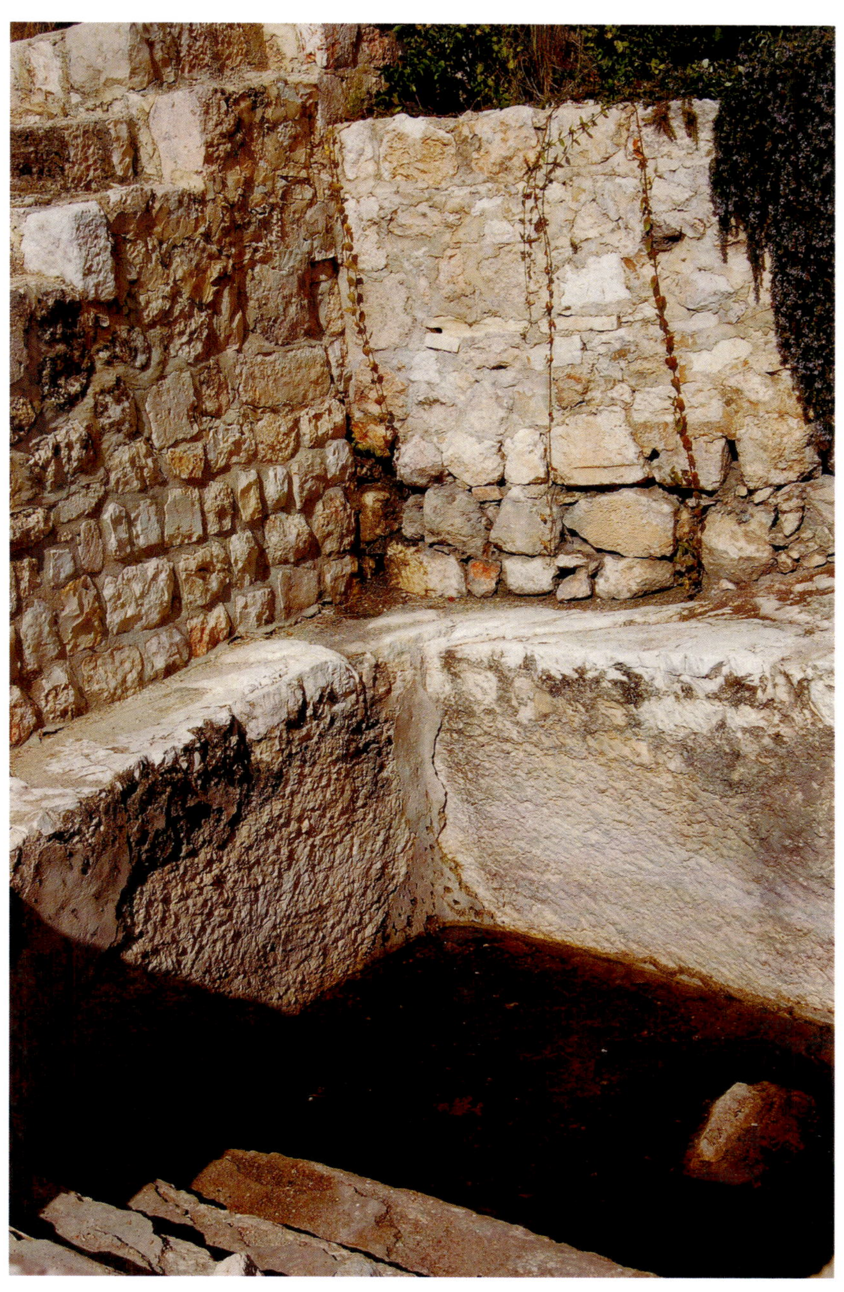

Old City, Jerusalem 2009

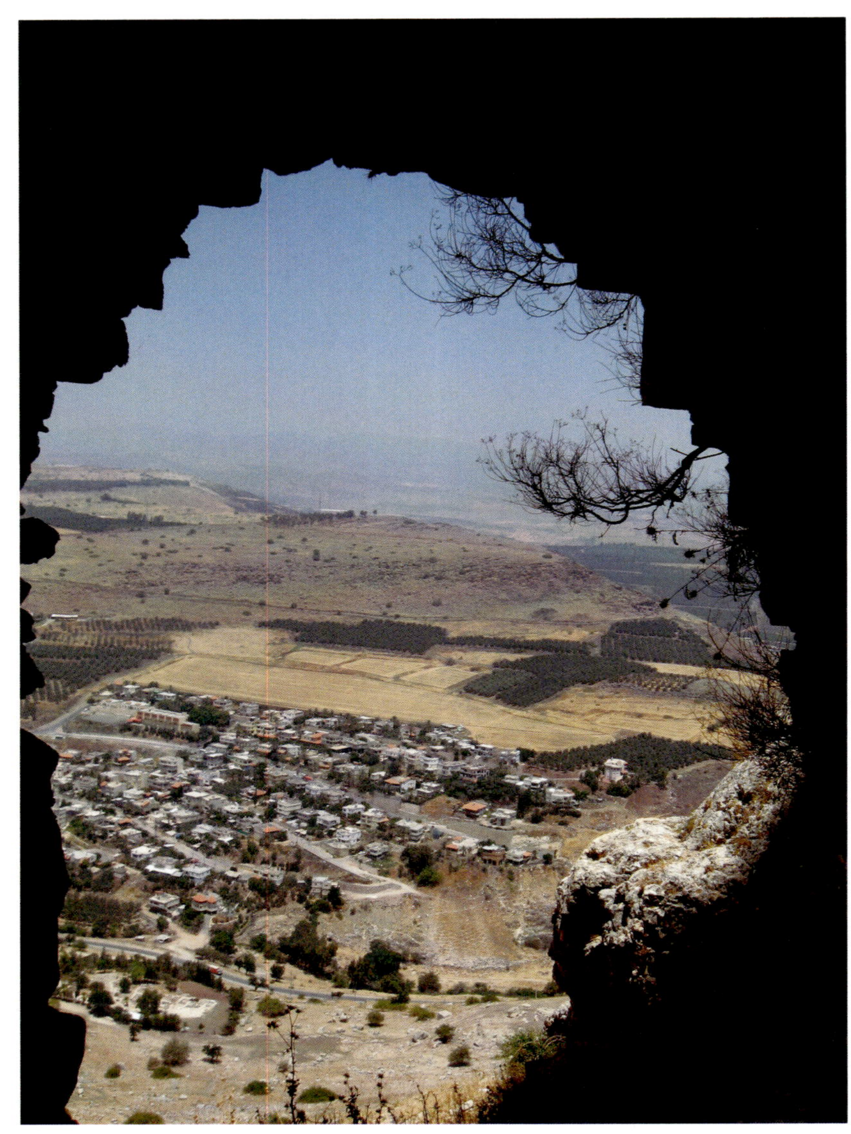

Galilee 2008

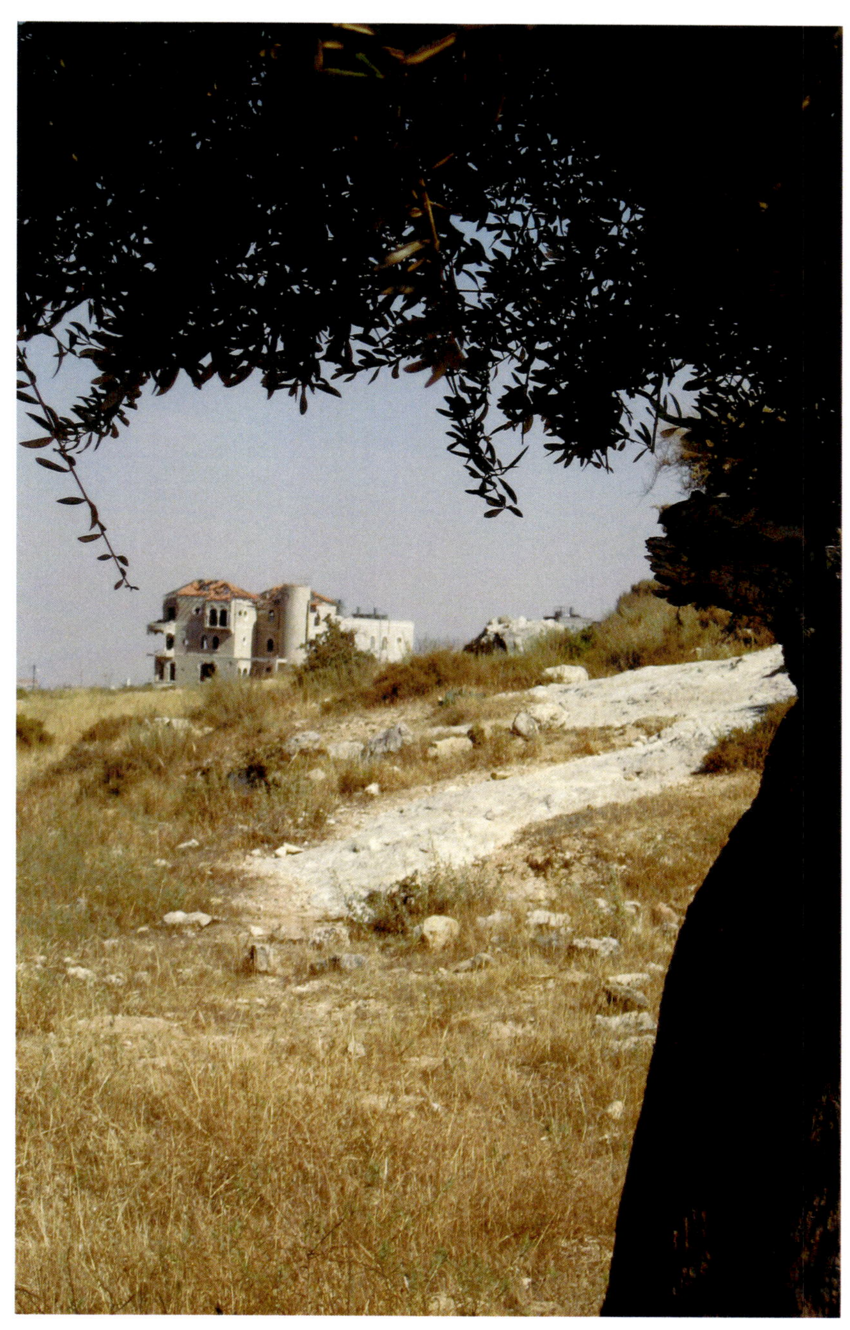

Beit Jala 2010

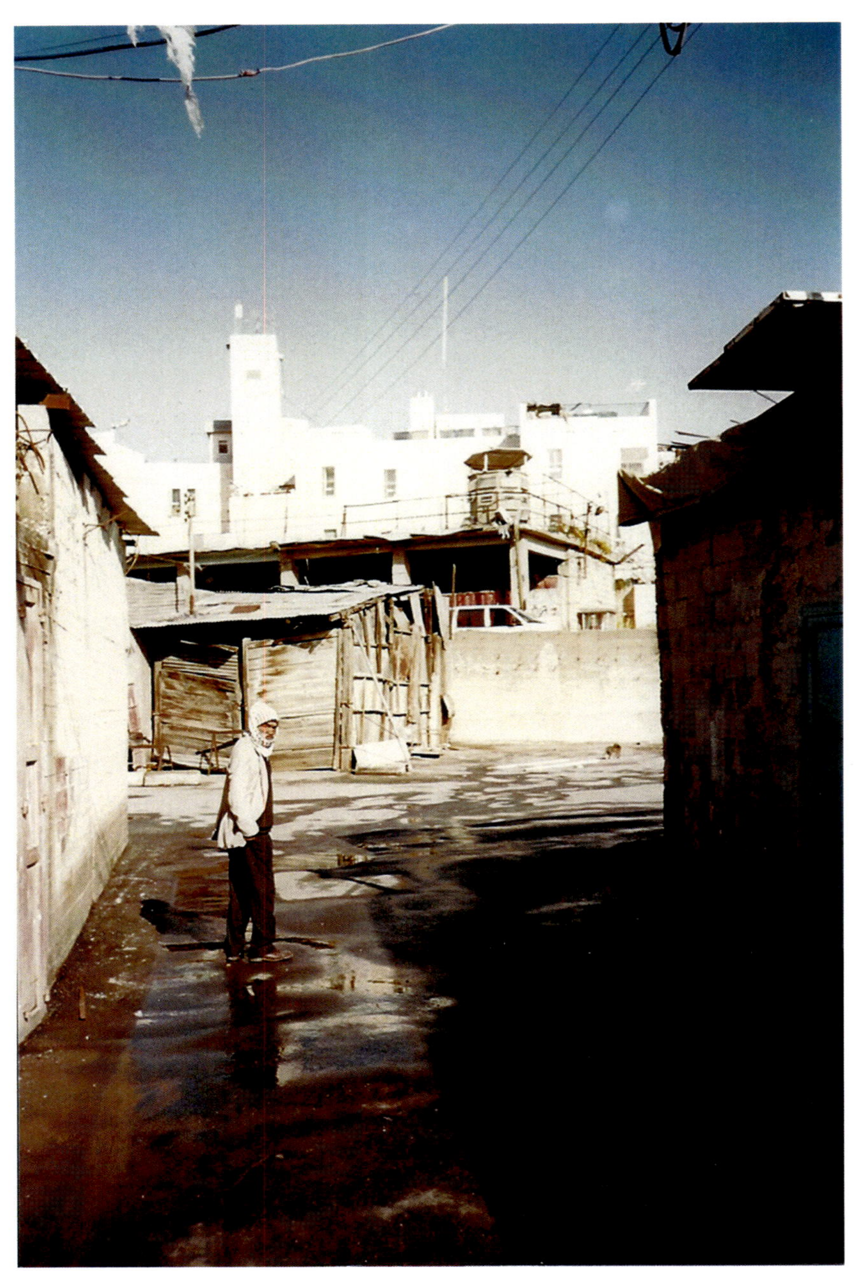

Hebron 2000

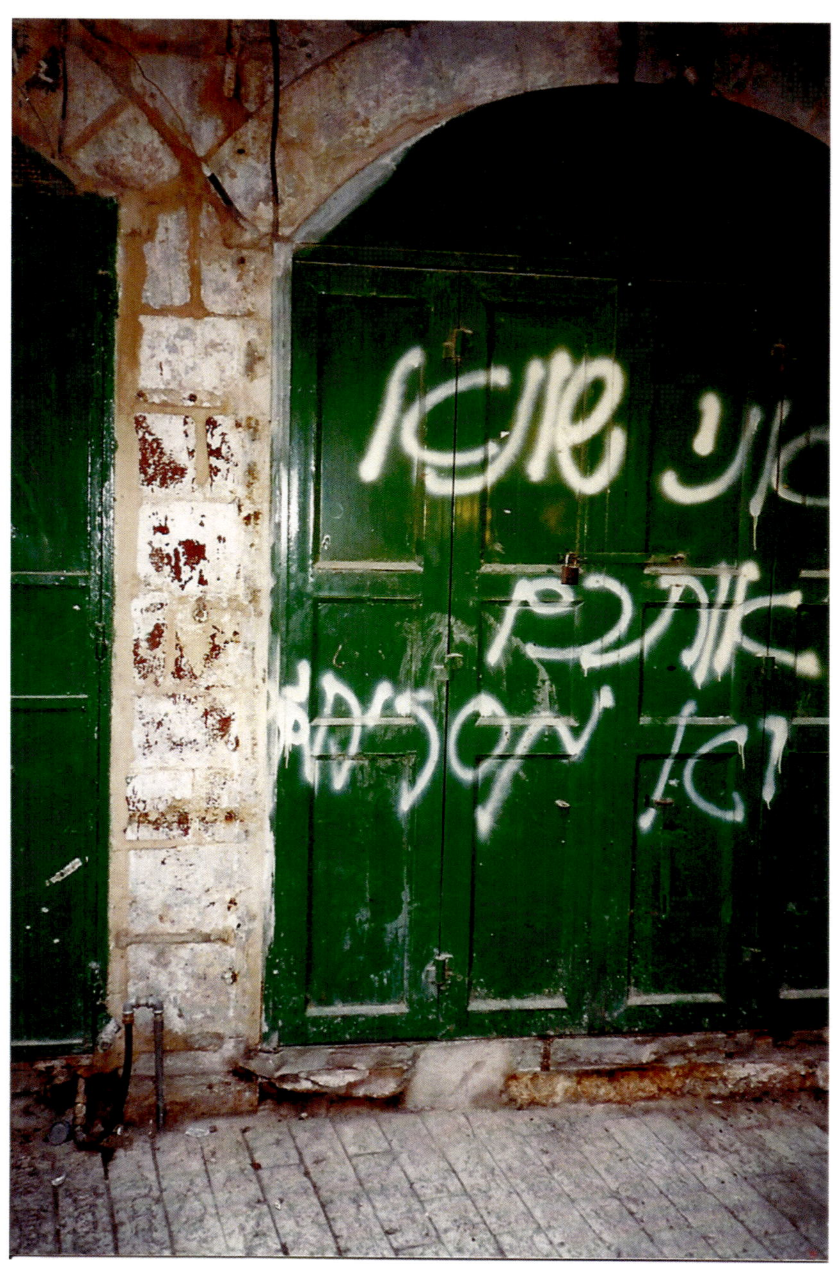

Hebron 2000

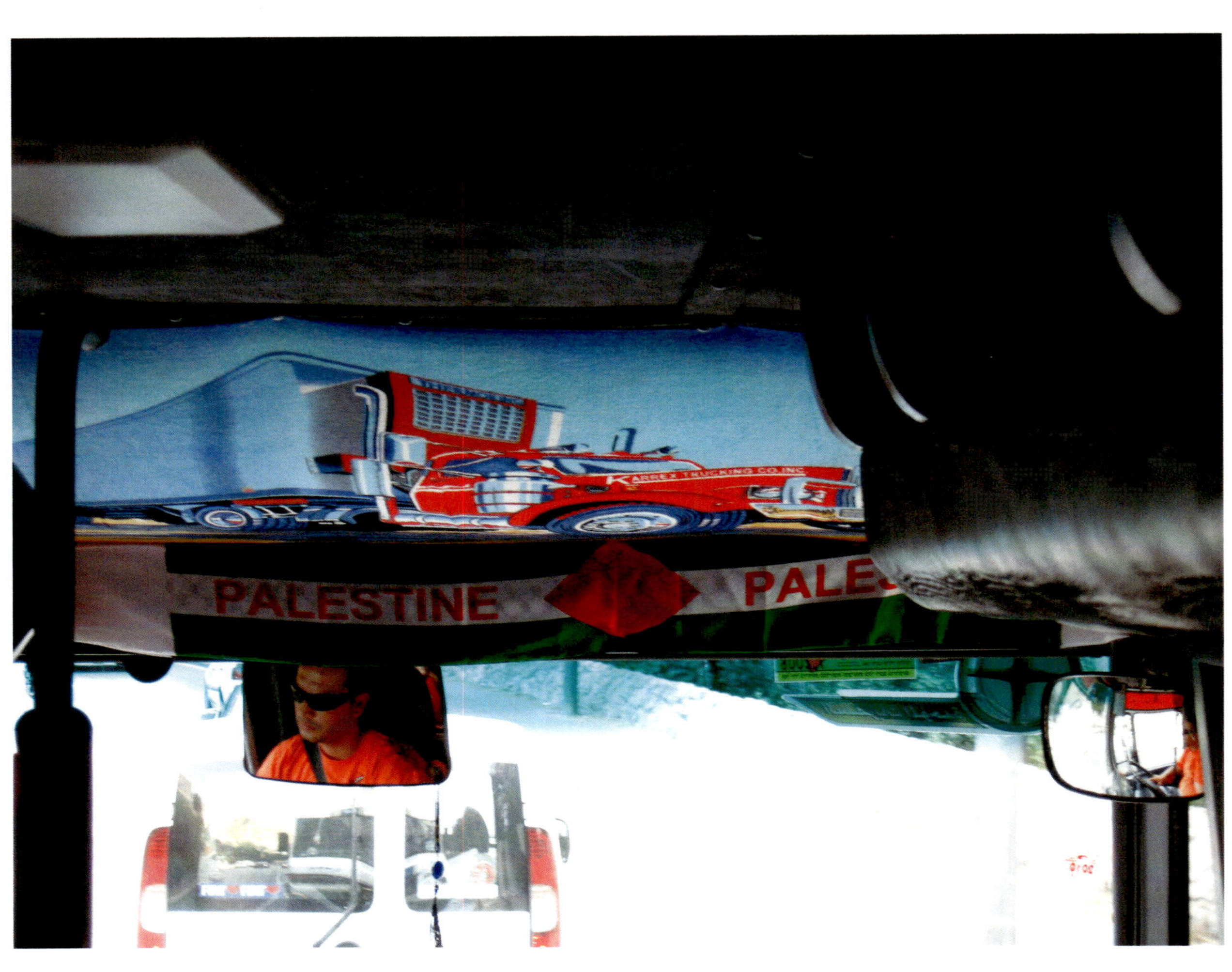

Jerusalem 2010

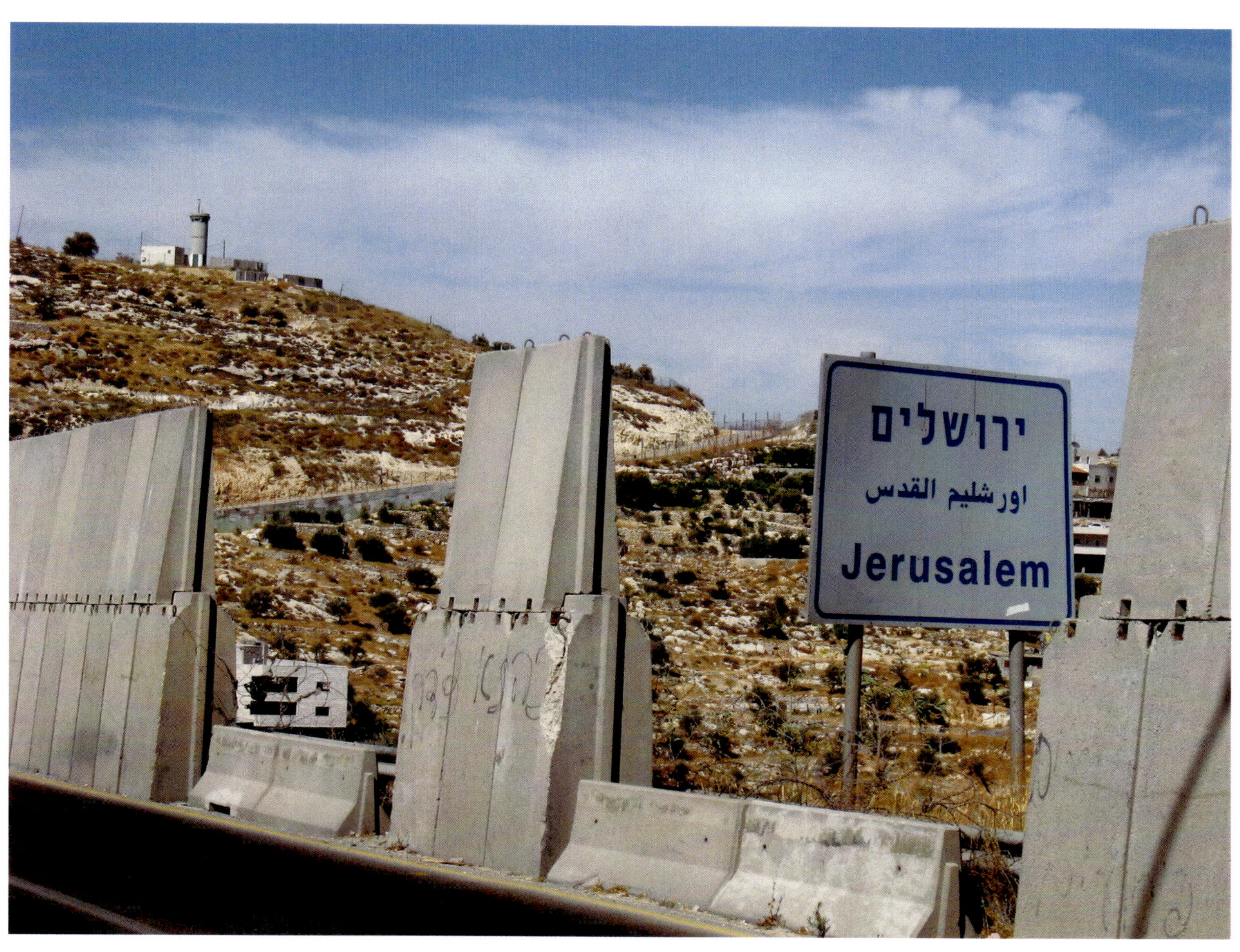

Green Line 2010

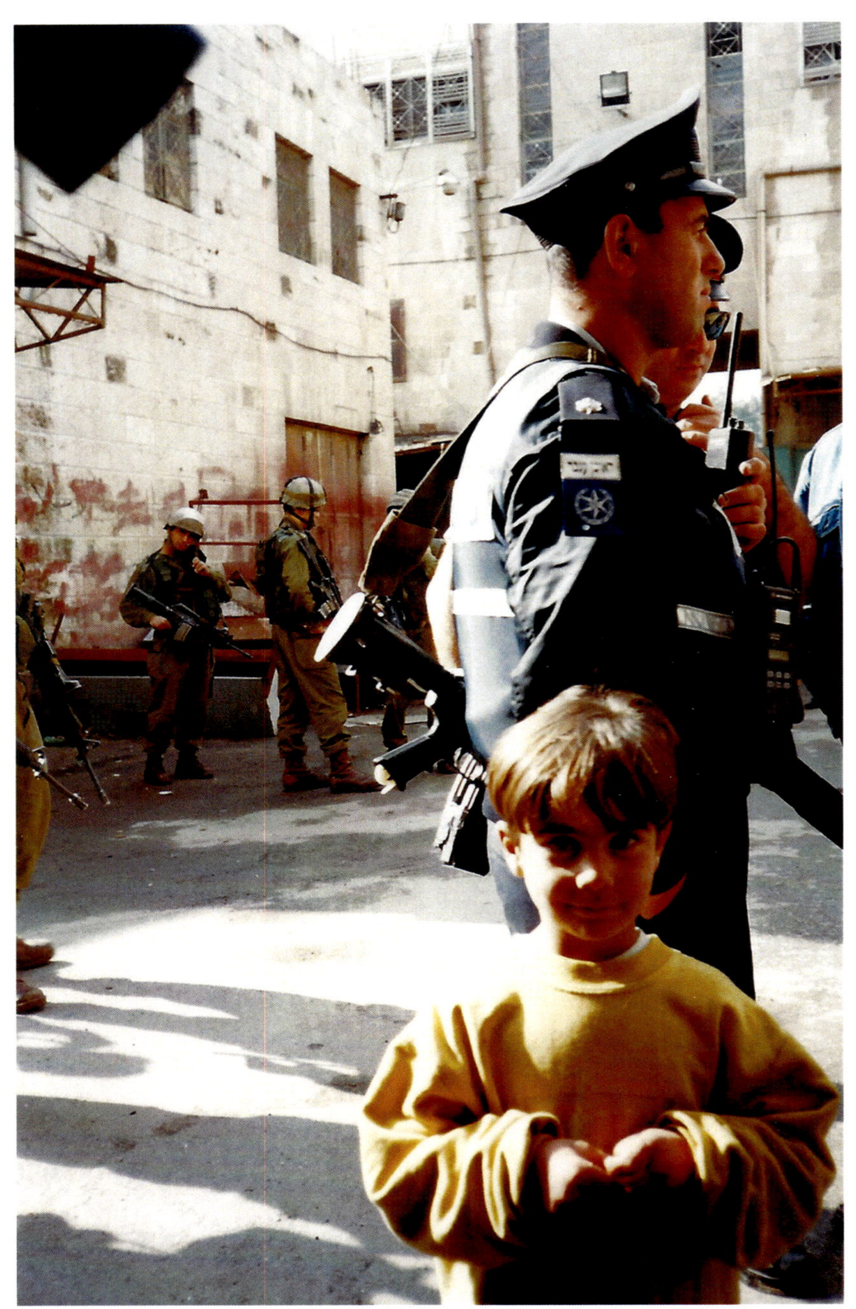

Hebron 2000

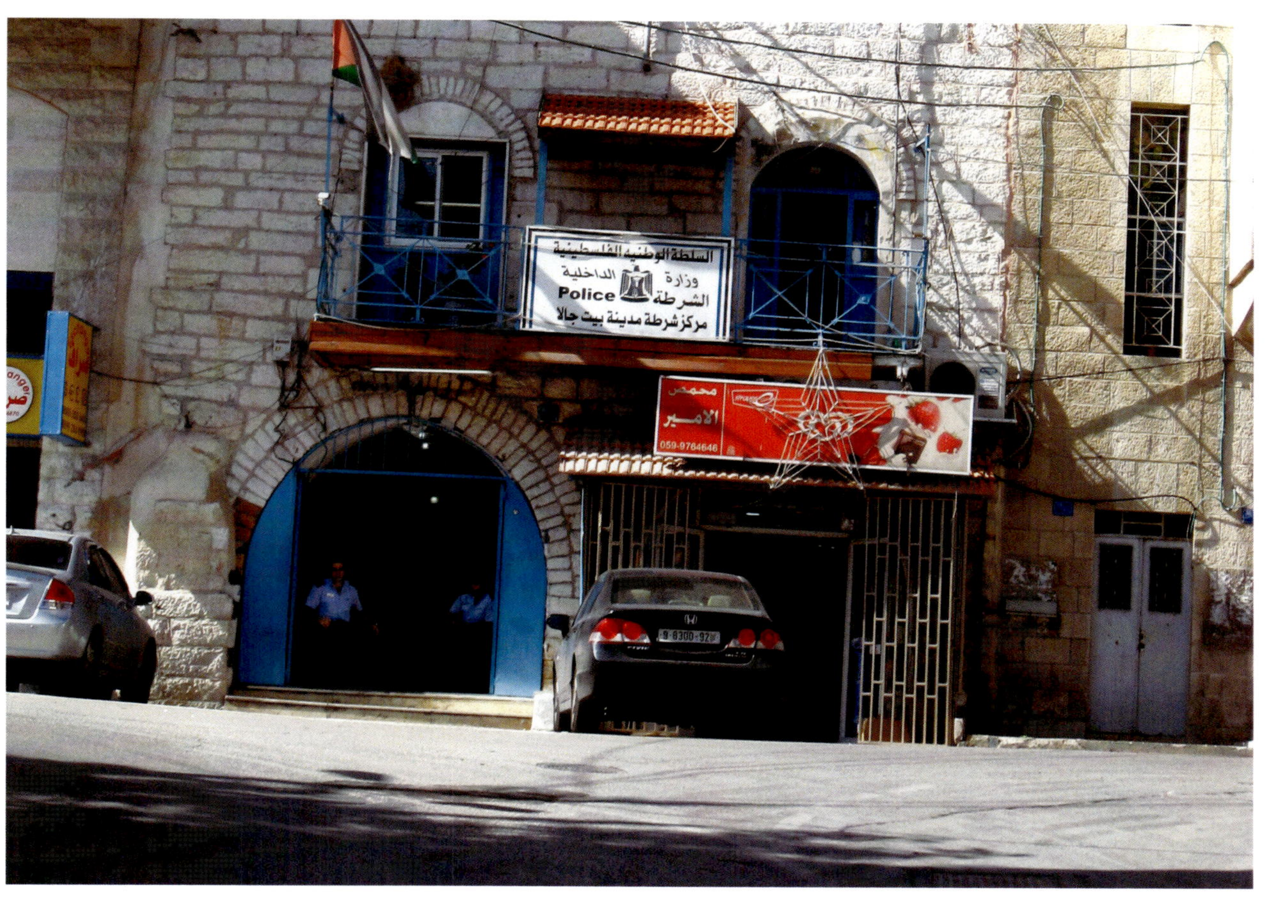

Beit Jala 2010

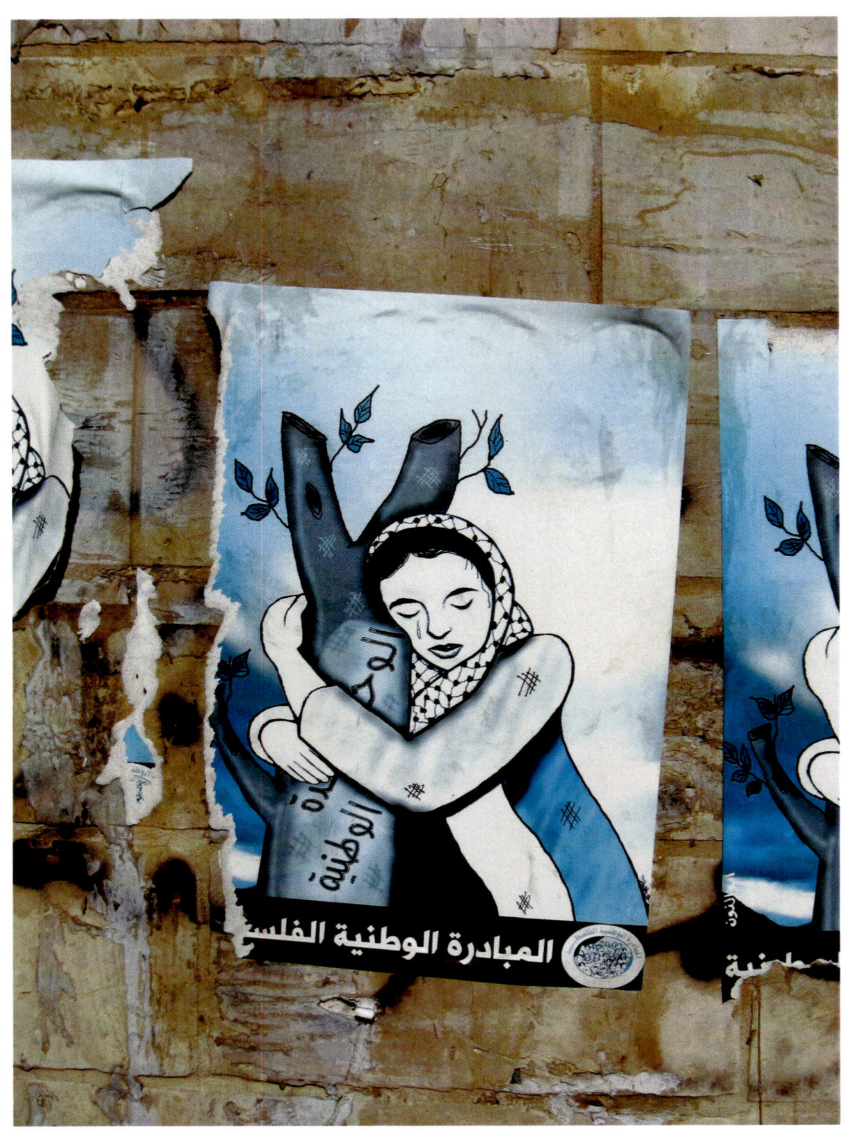

Bethlehem 2010

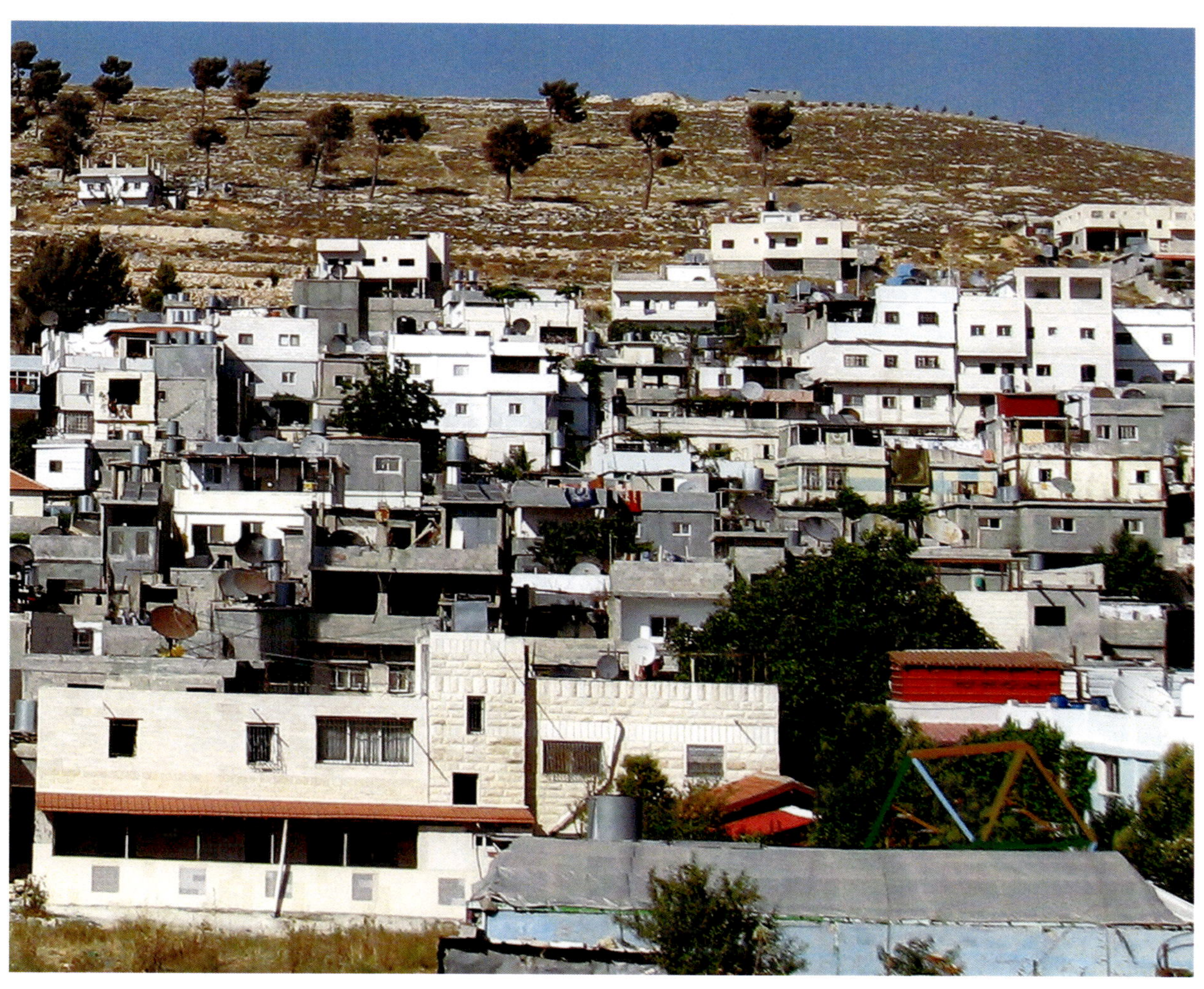

El Arroub 2010

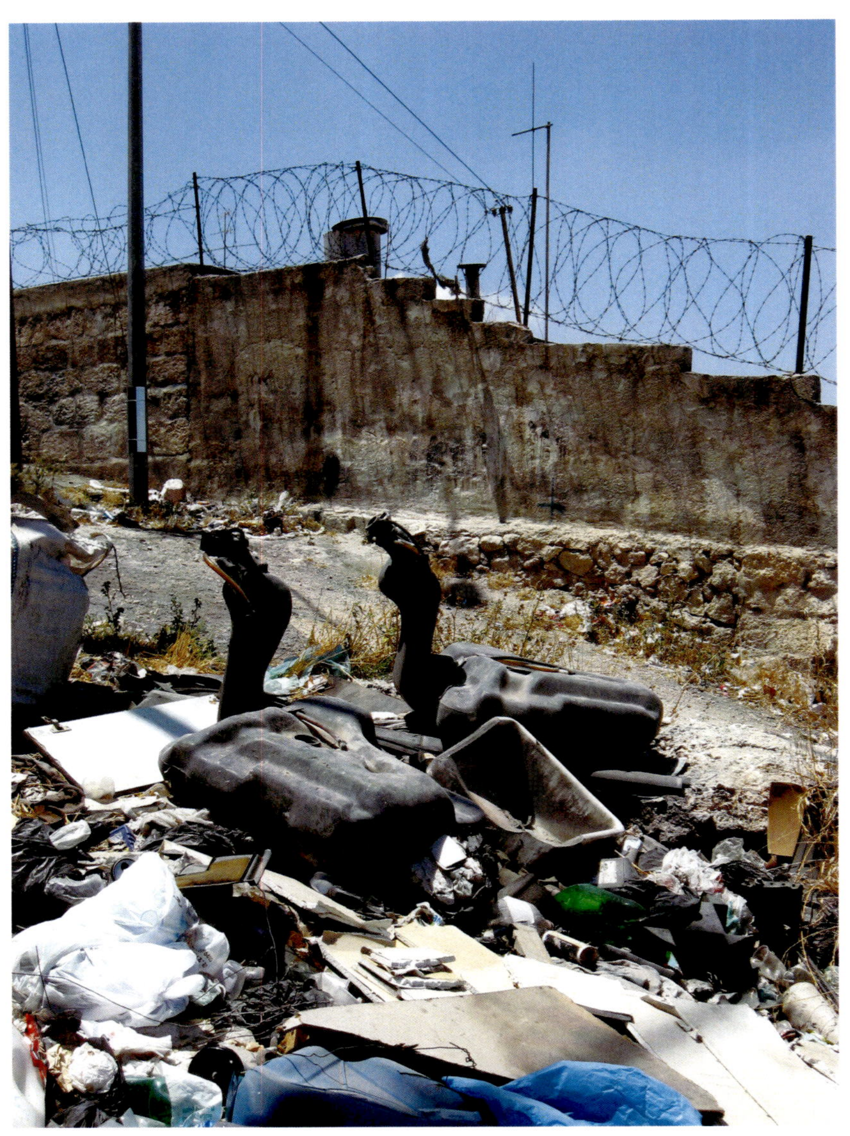

Bethlehem 2010

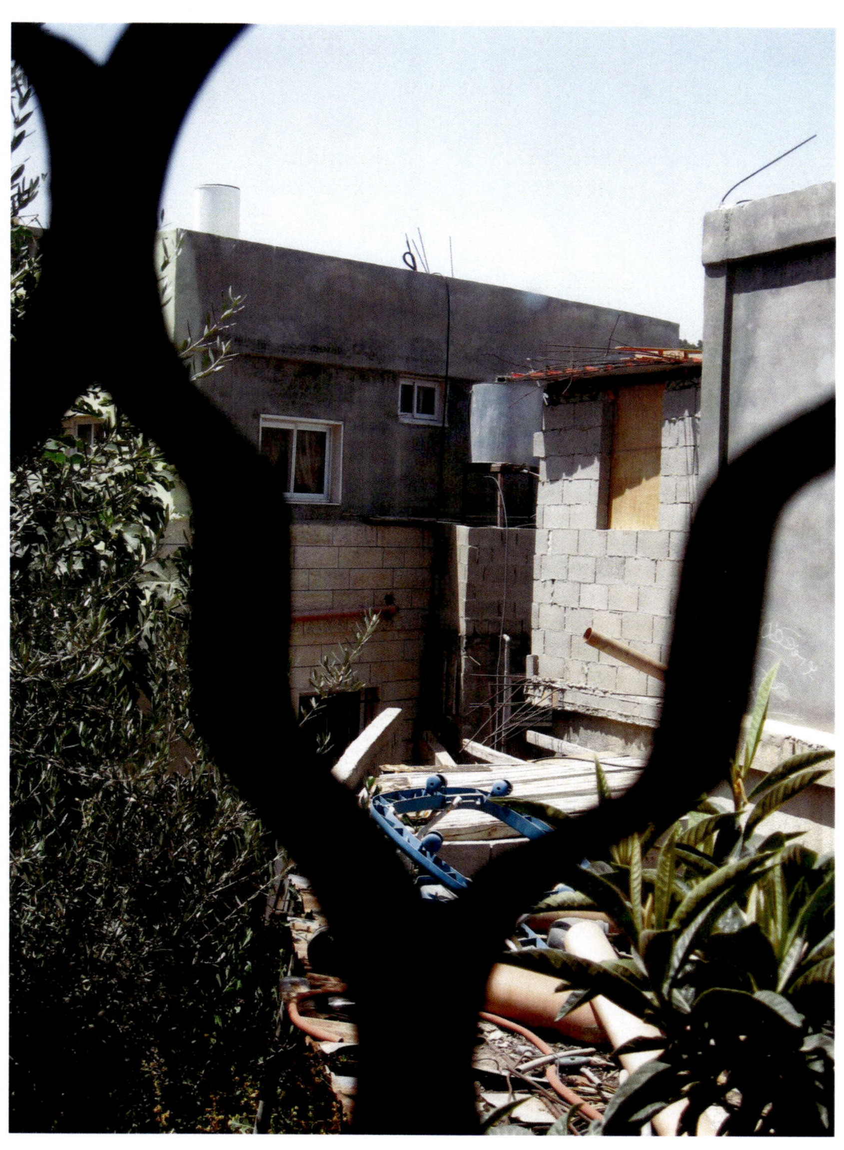

El Arroub 2010

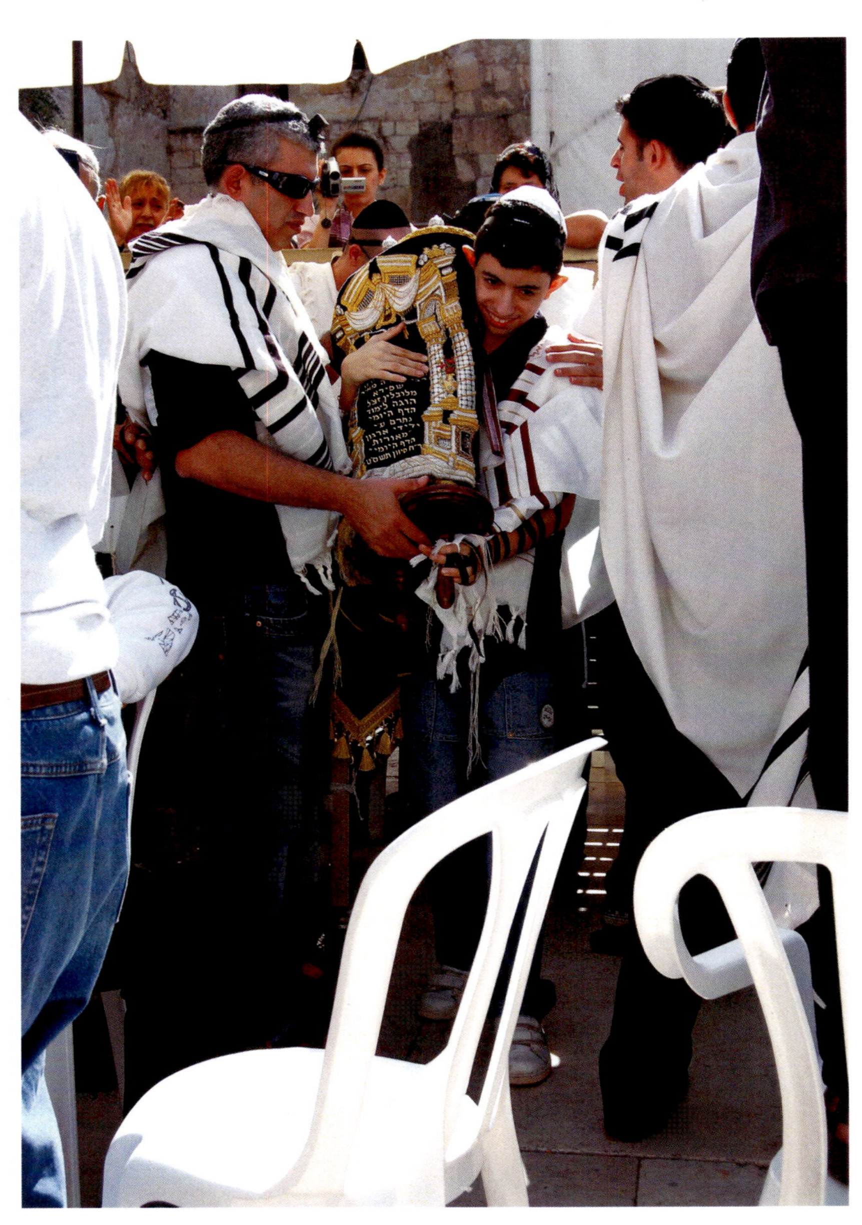

Old City, Jerusalem 2009

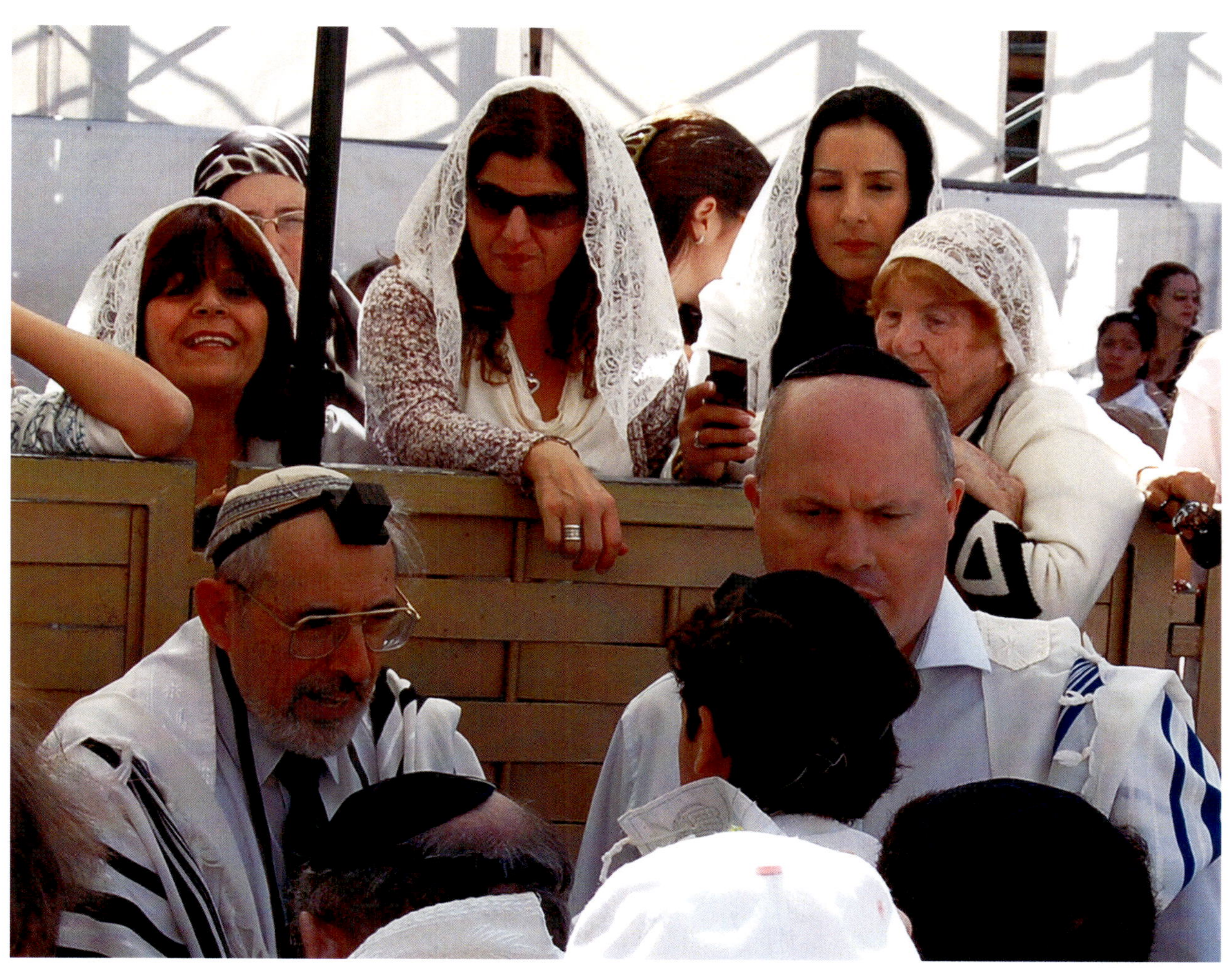

Old City, Jerusalem 2009

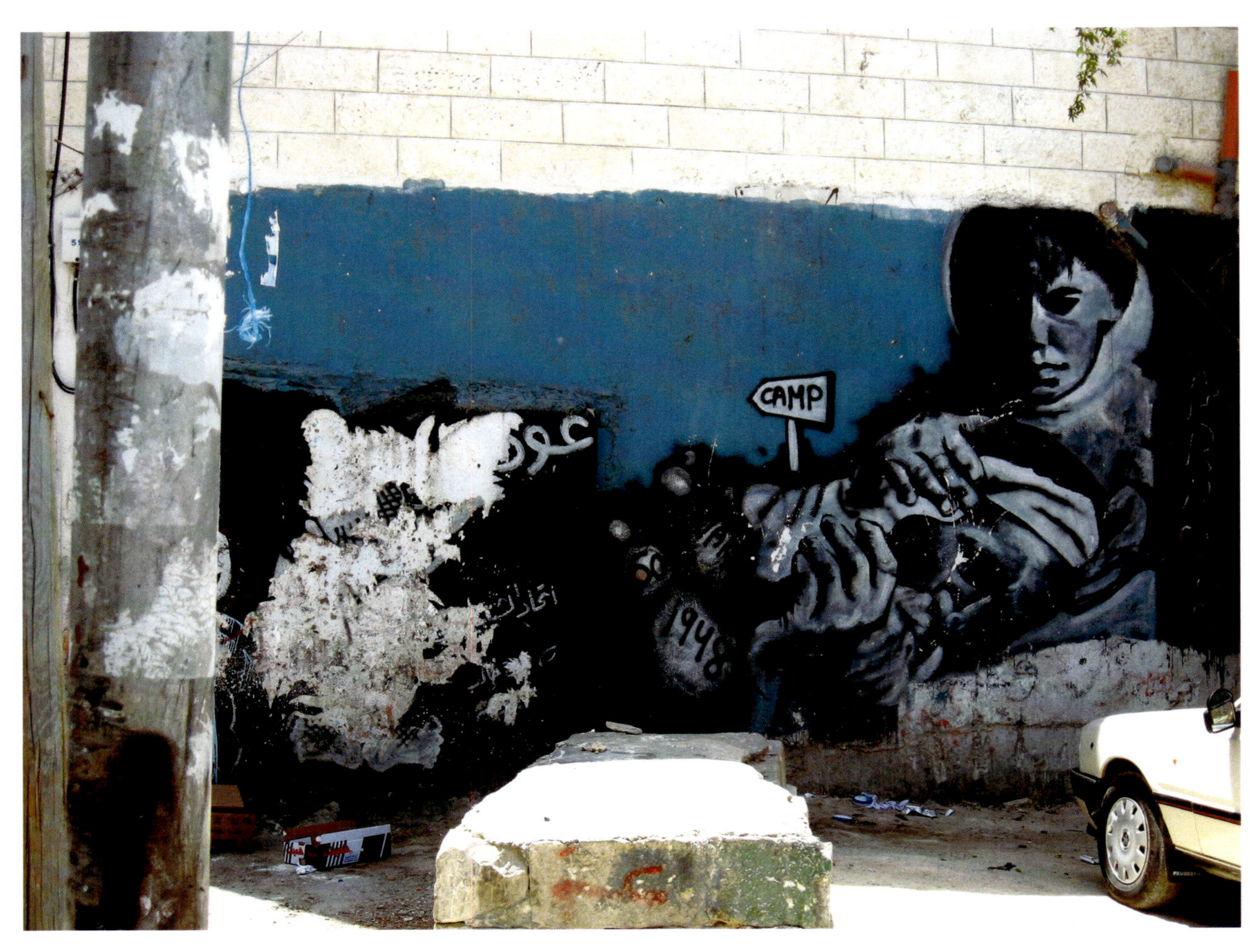

El Arroub 2010

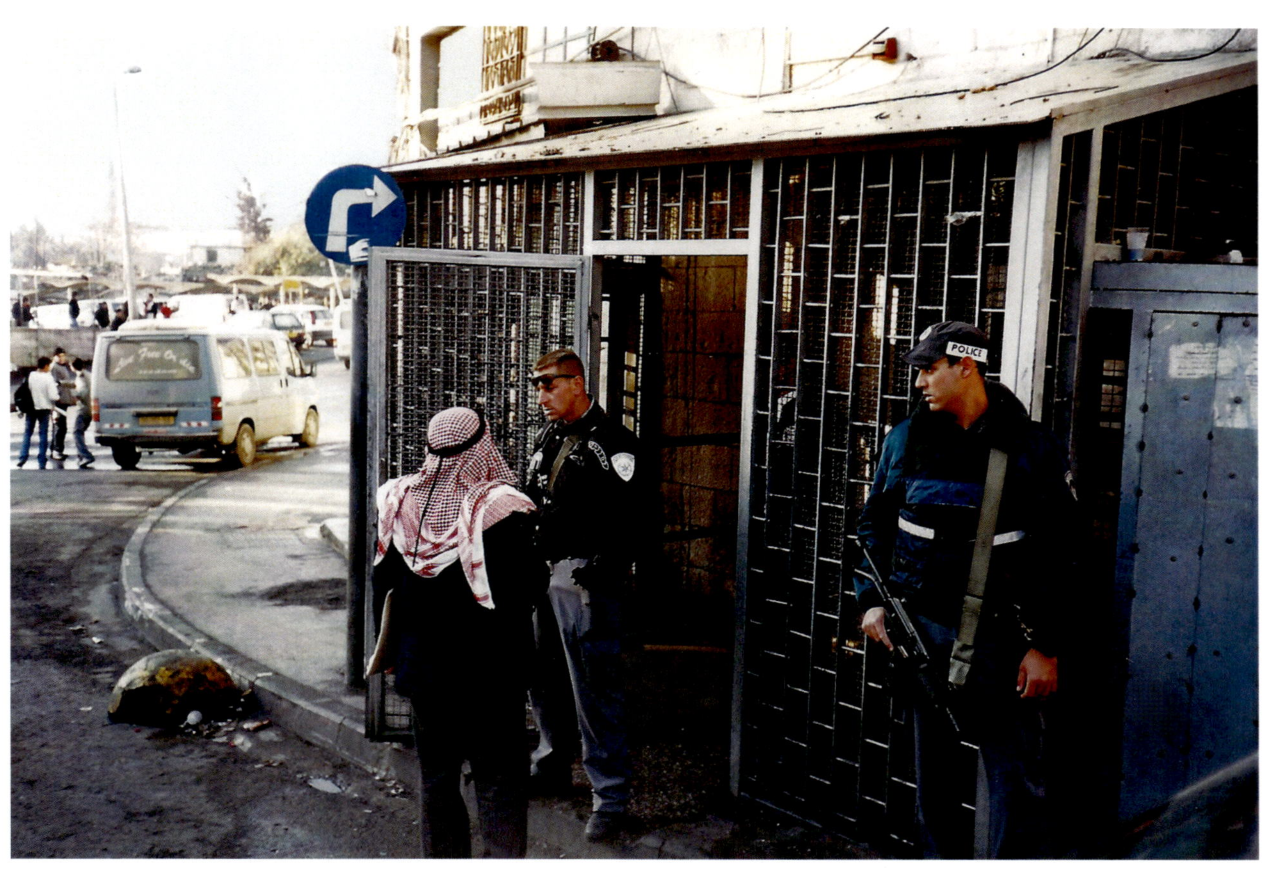

Jerusalem 2000

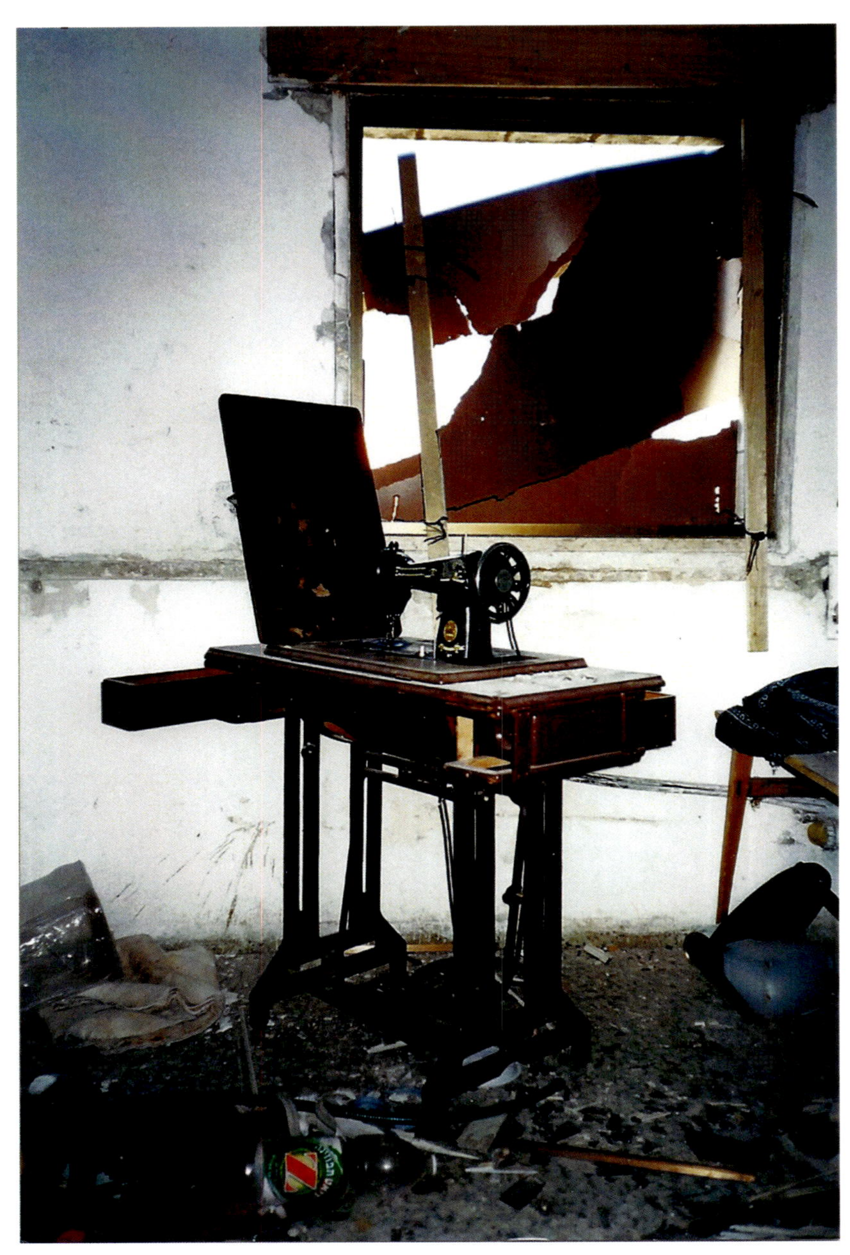

Beit Jala 2000

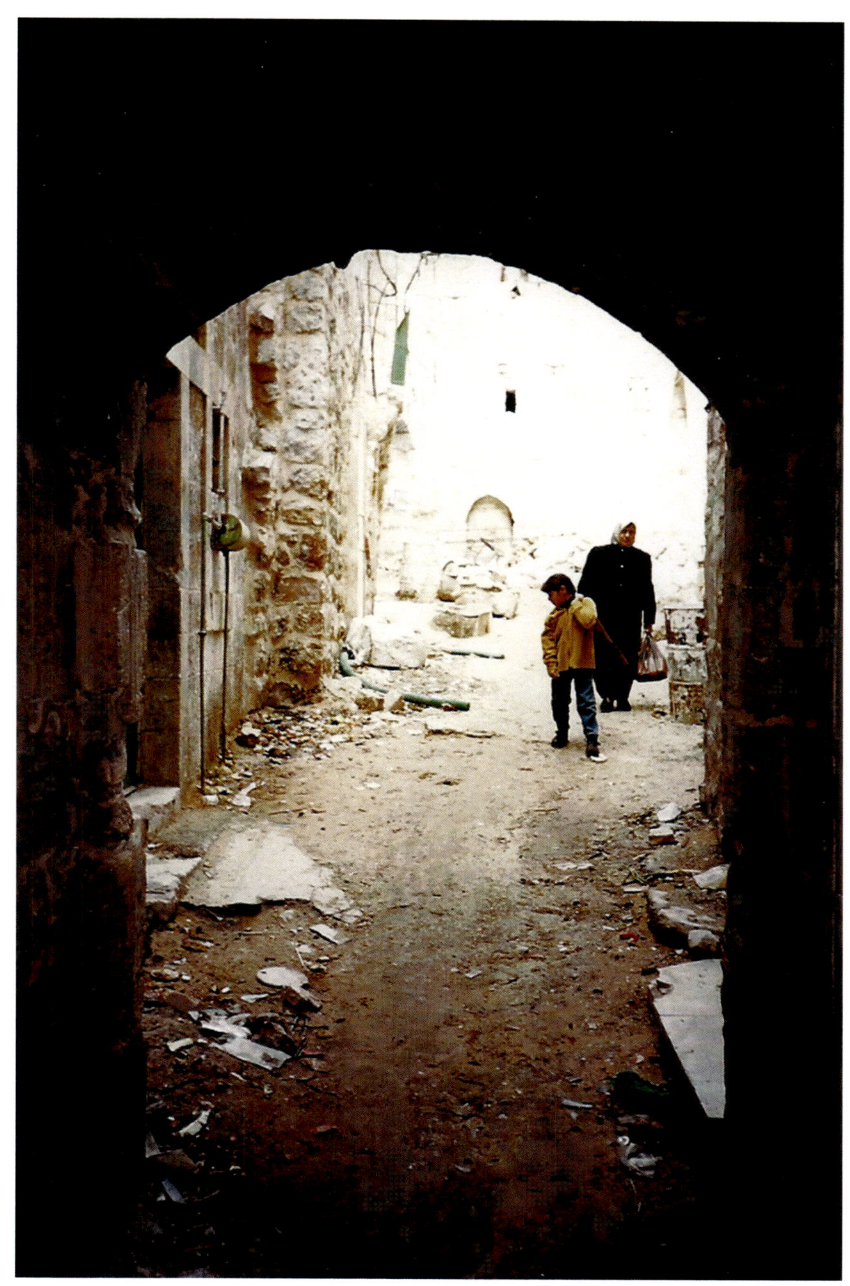

Hebron 2000

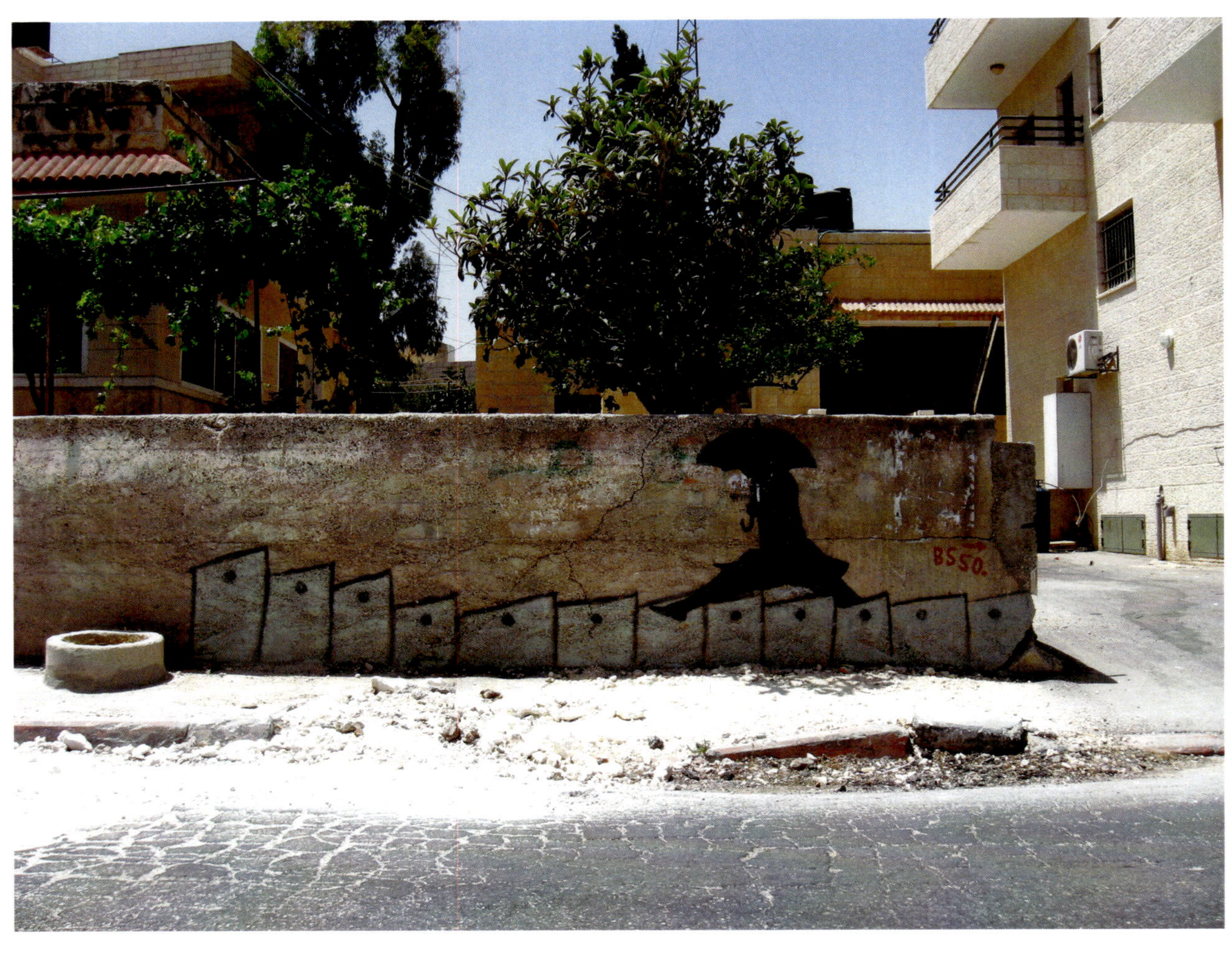

Beit Sahour 2010

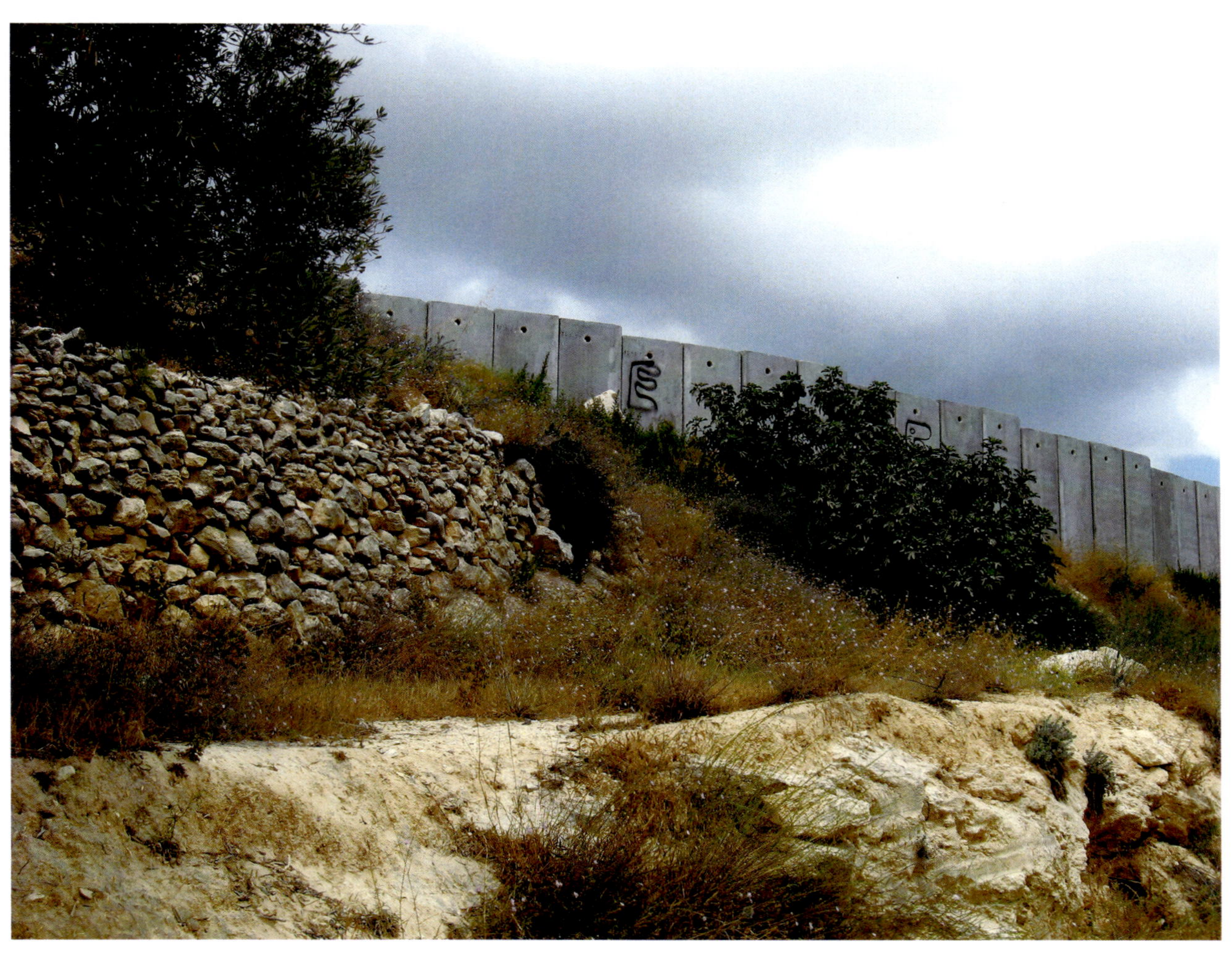

Separation Wall 2010

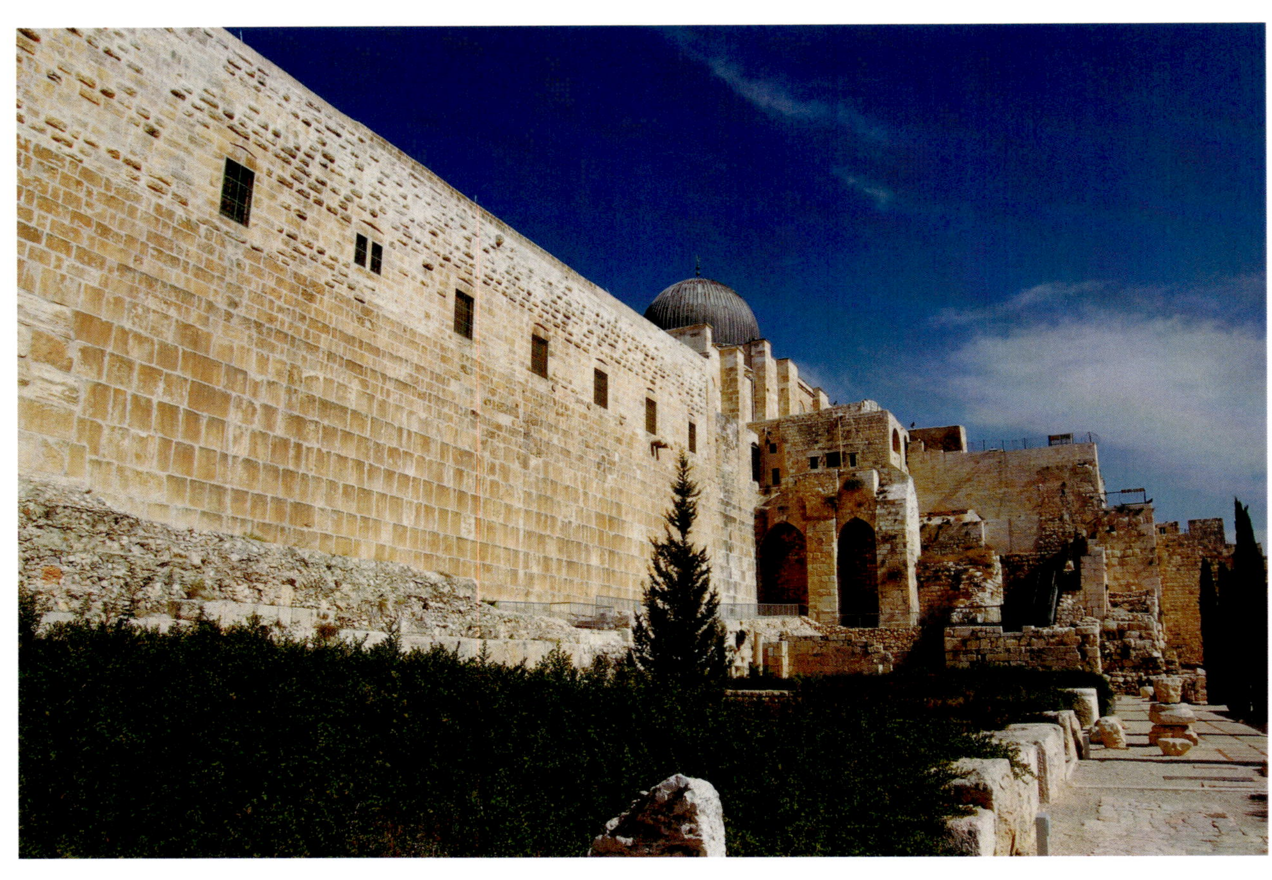

Old City, Jerusalem 2009

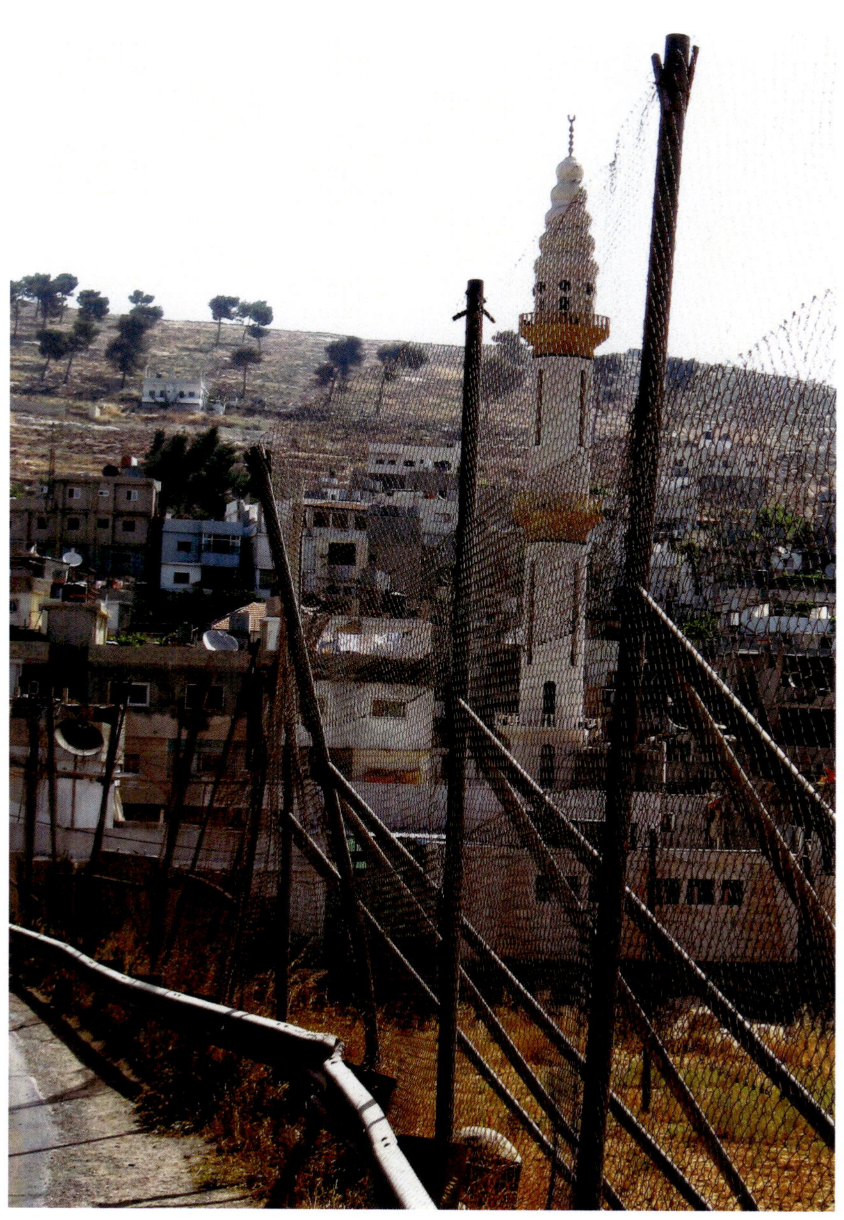

El Arroub 2010

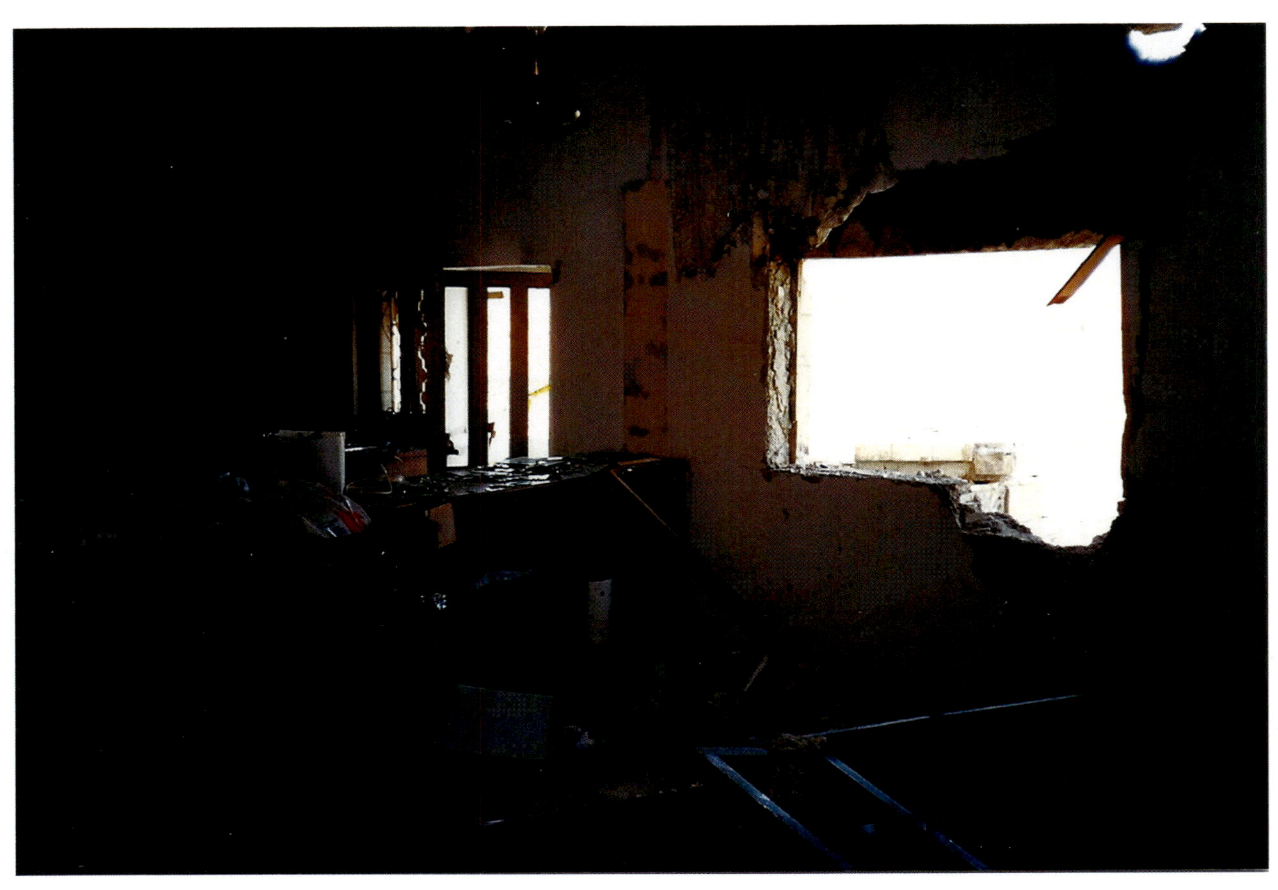

Beit Jala 2000

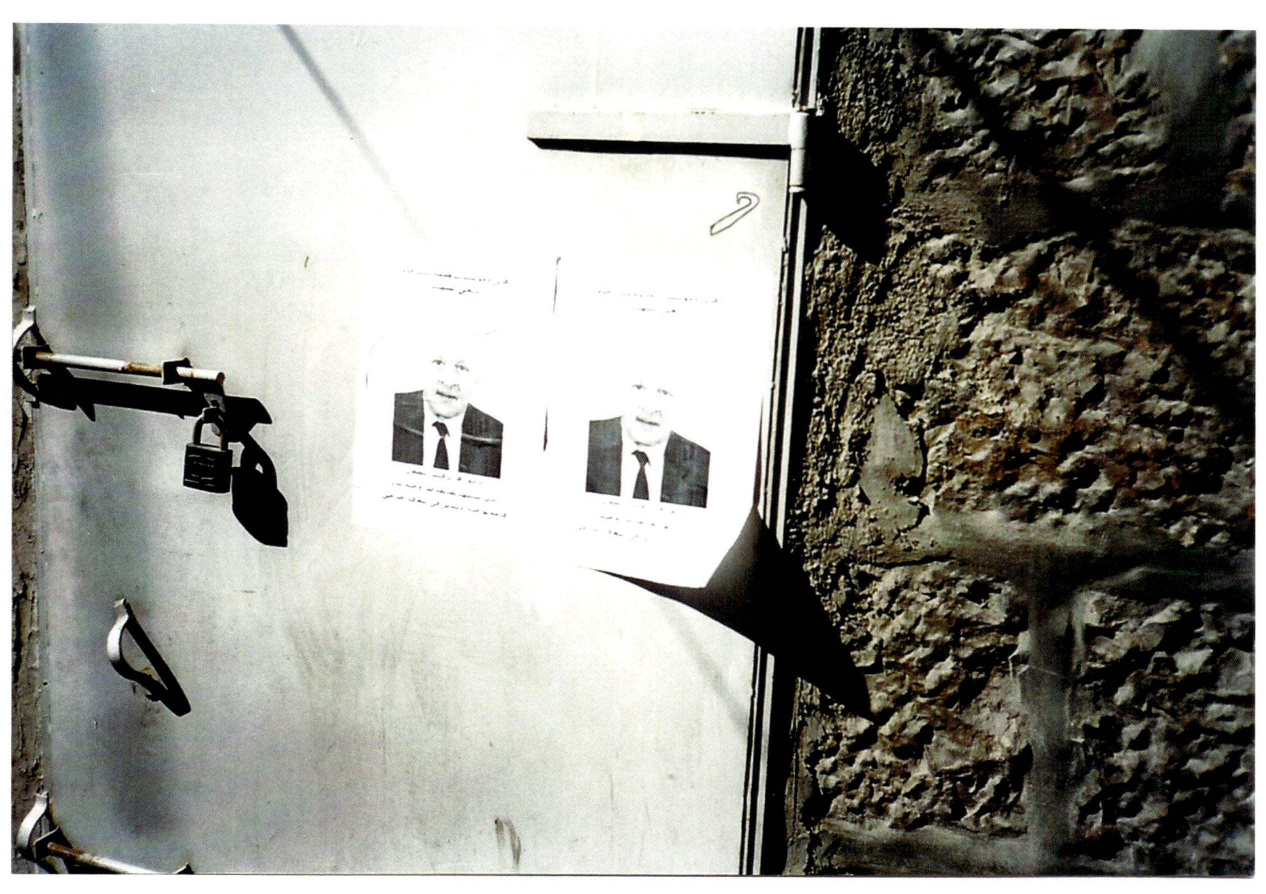

Beit Jala 2000

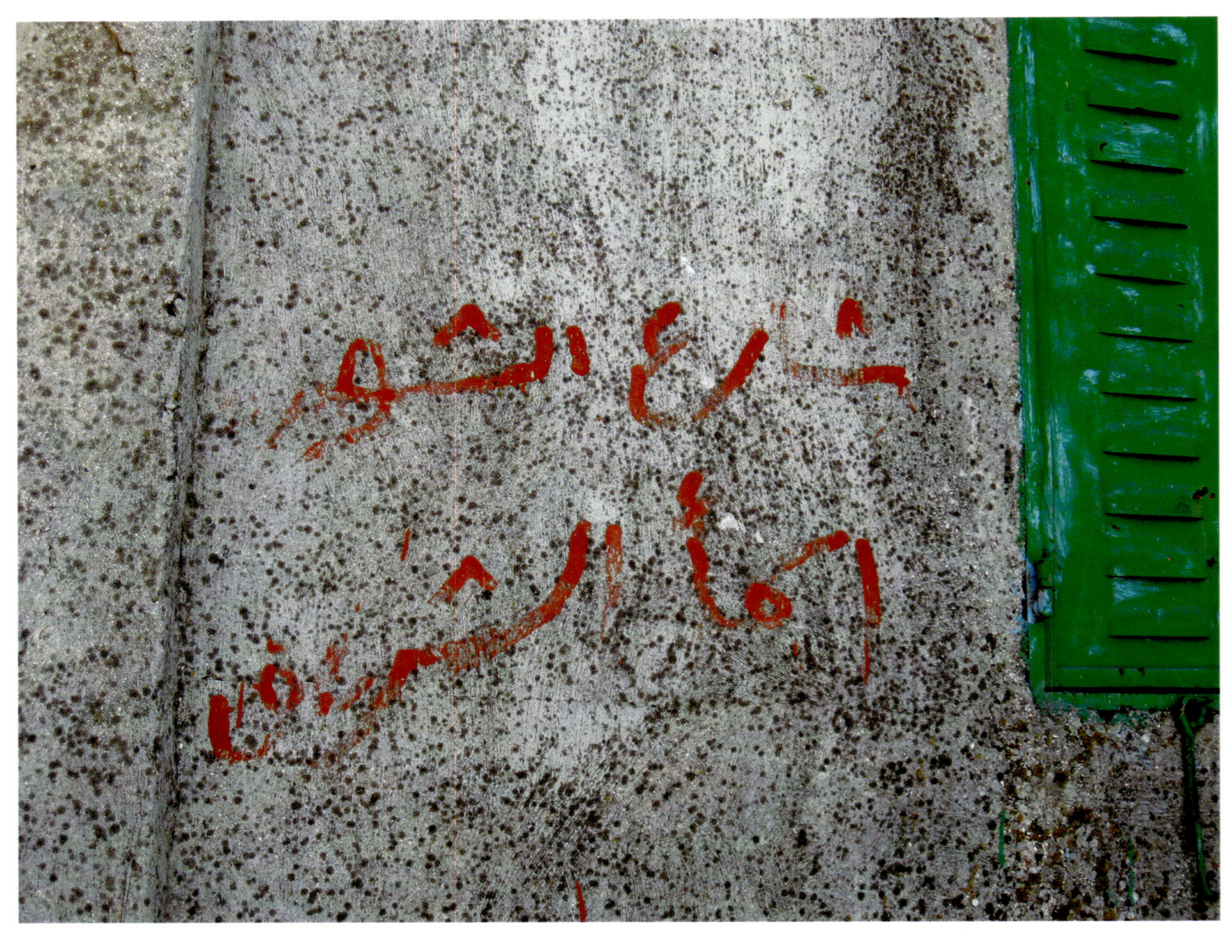

El Arroub 2010

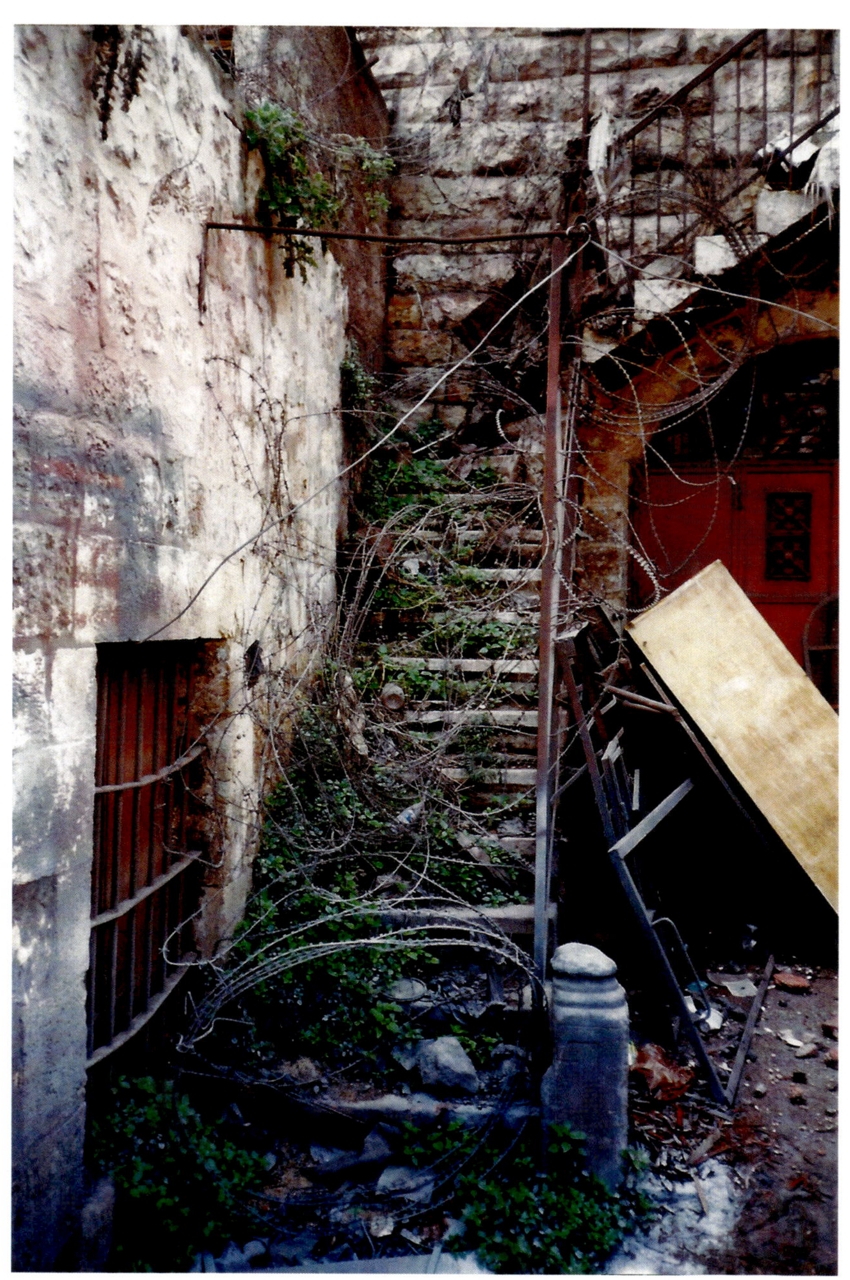

Hebron 2000

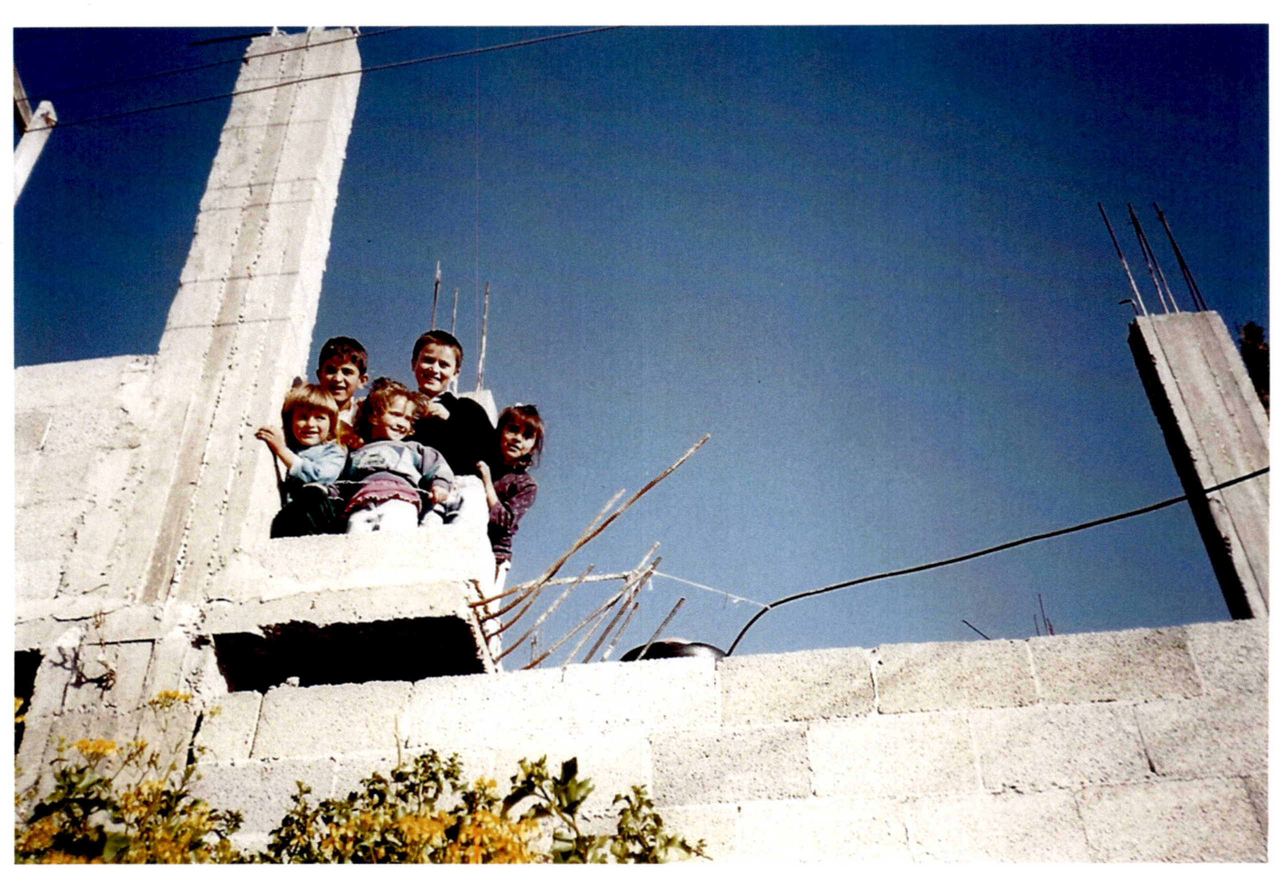

Hebron 2000

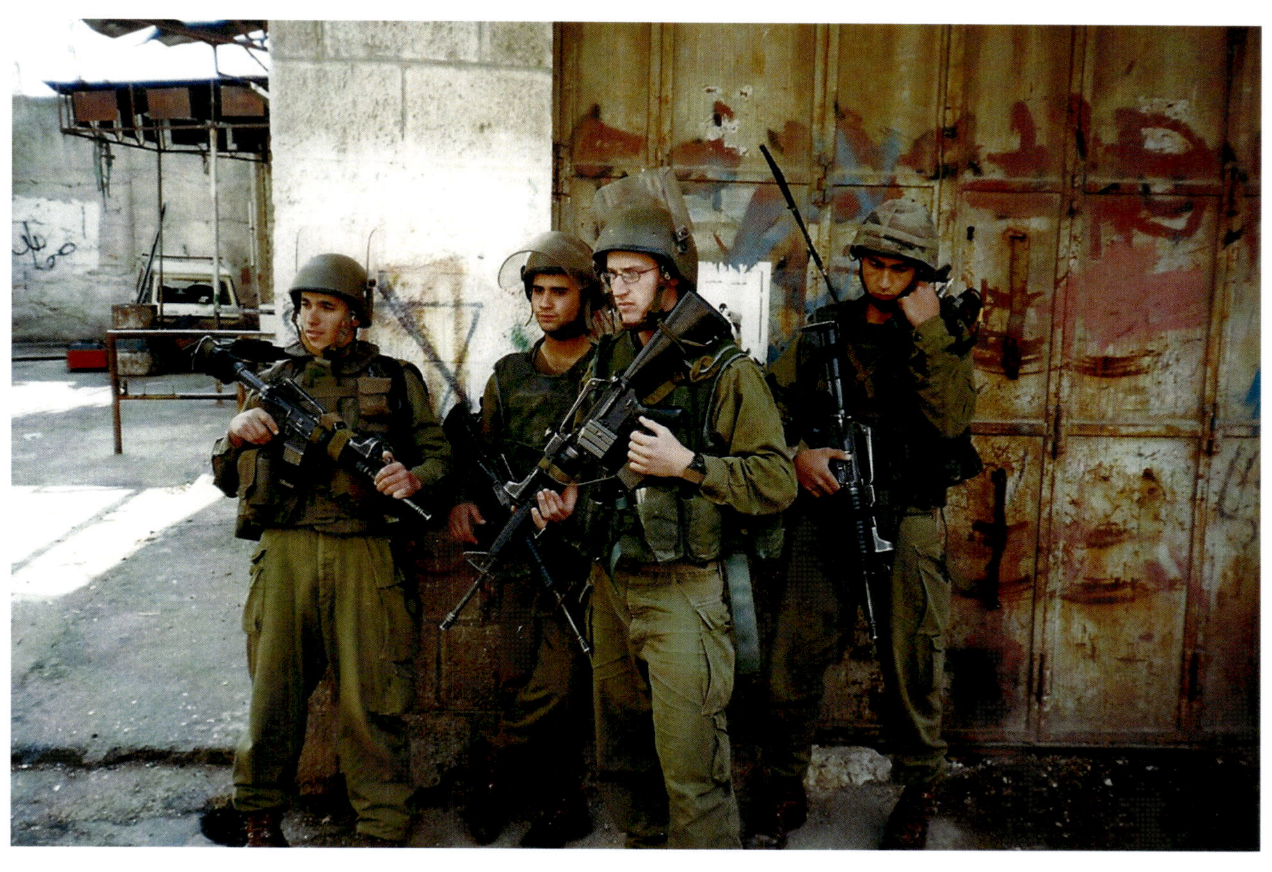

Hebron 2000

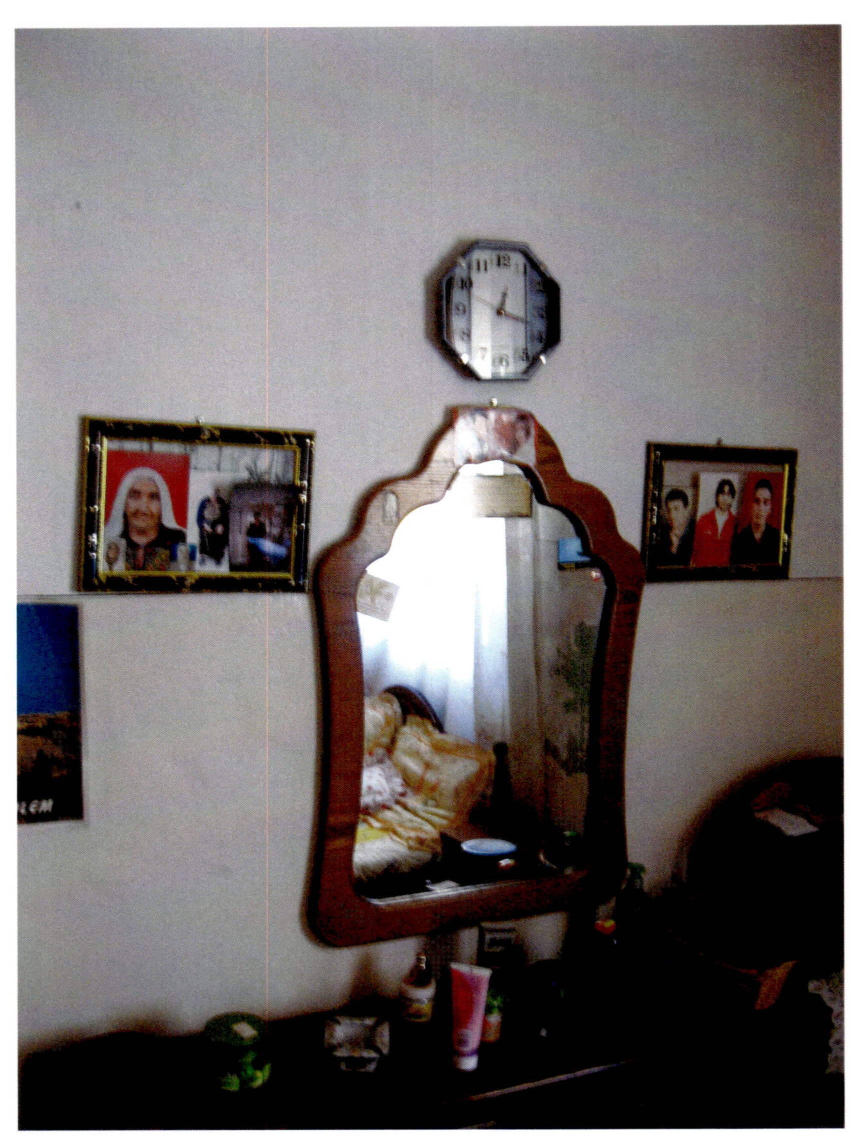

El Arroub 2010

56

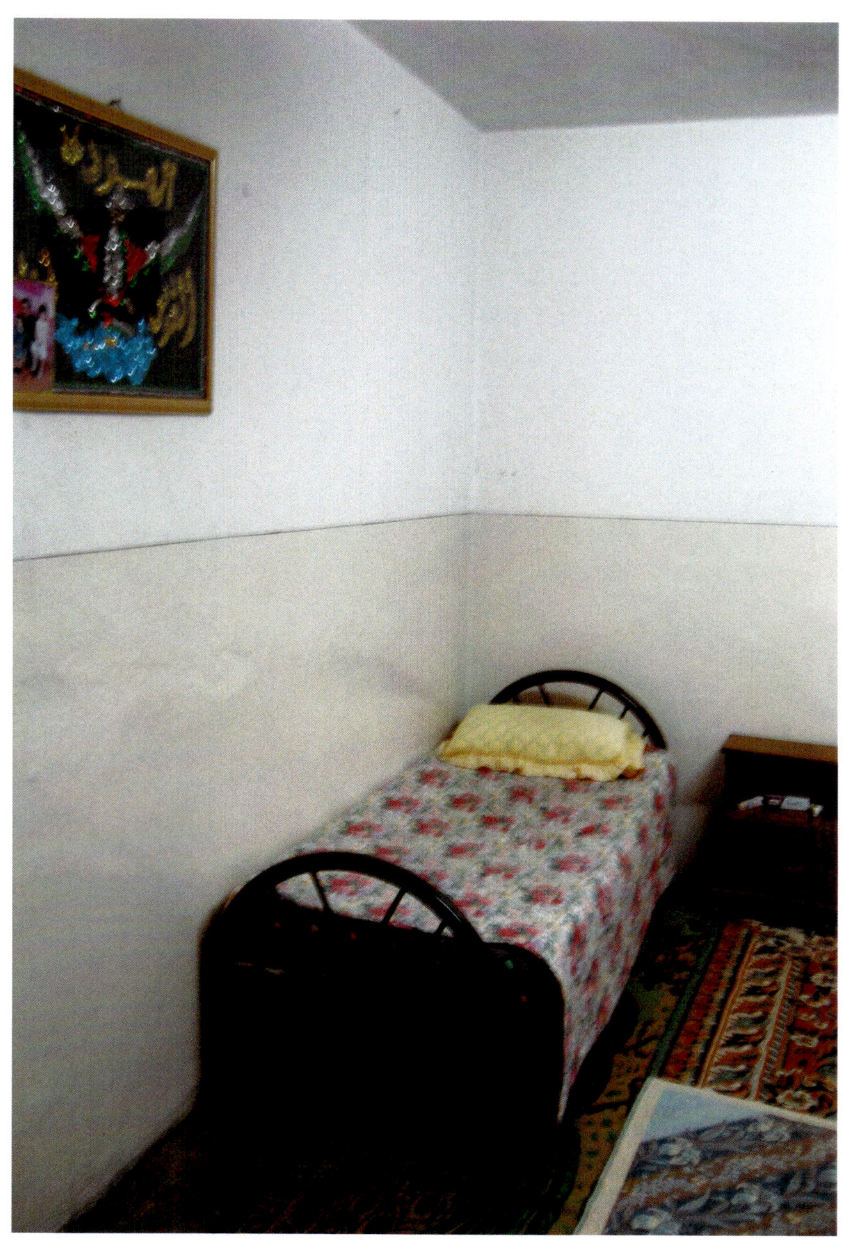

El Arroub 2010

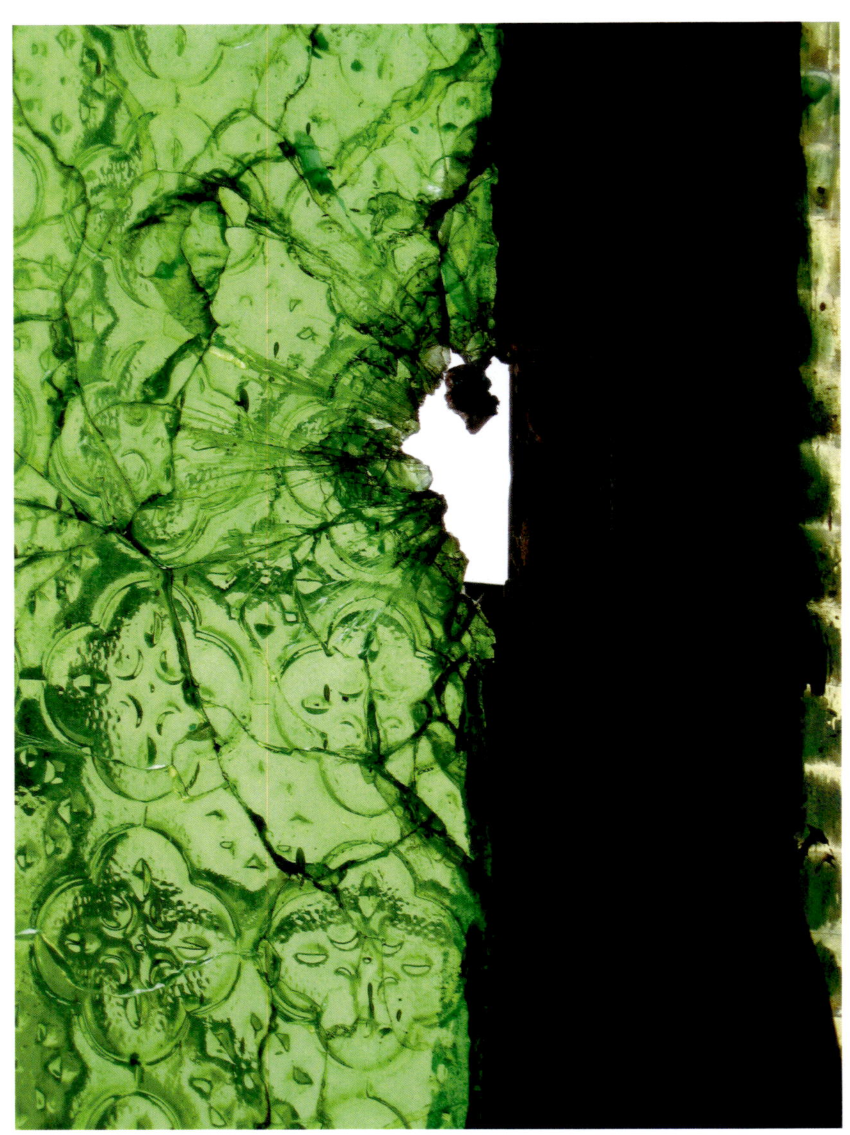

El Arroub 2010

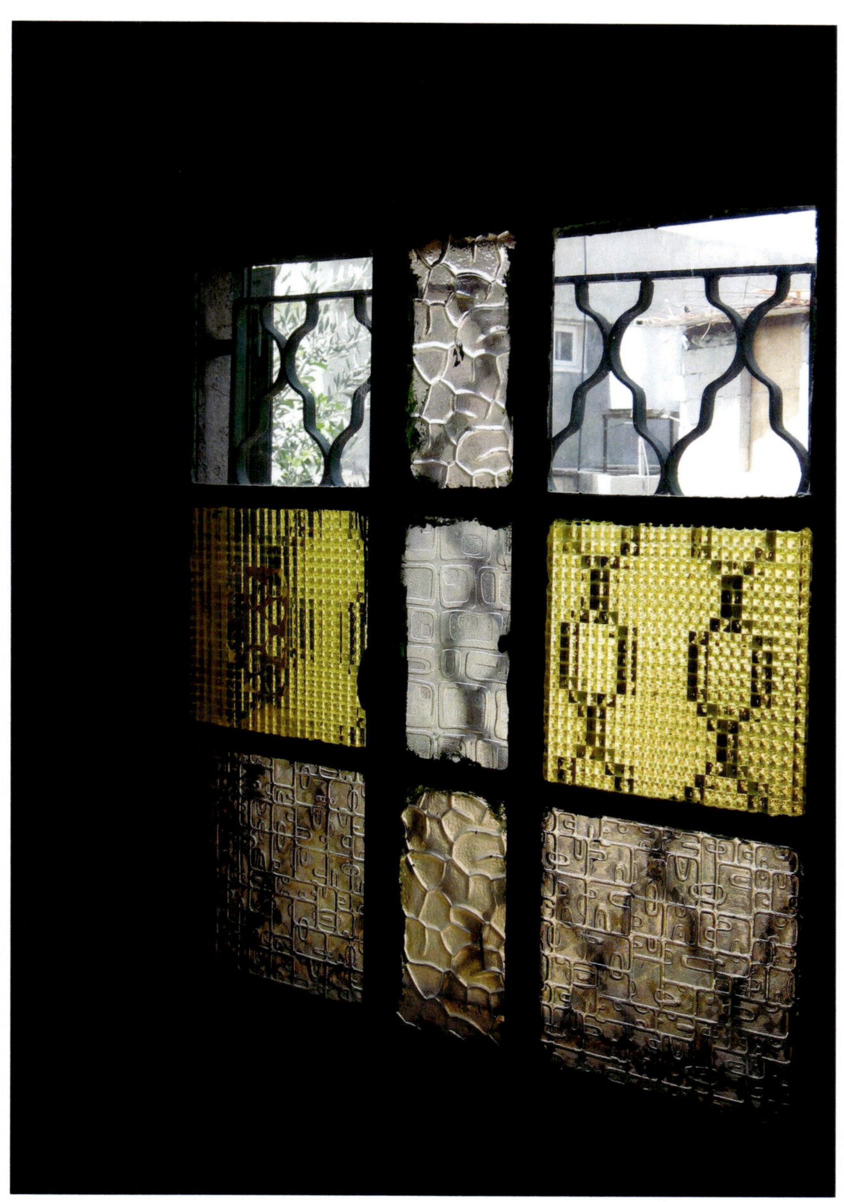

El Arroub 2010

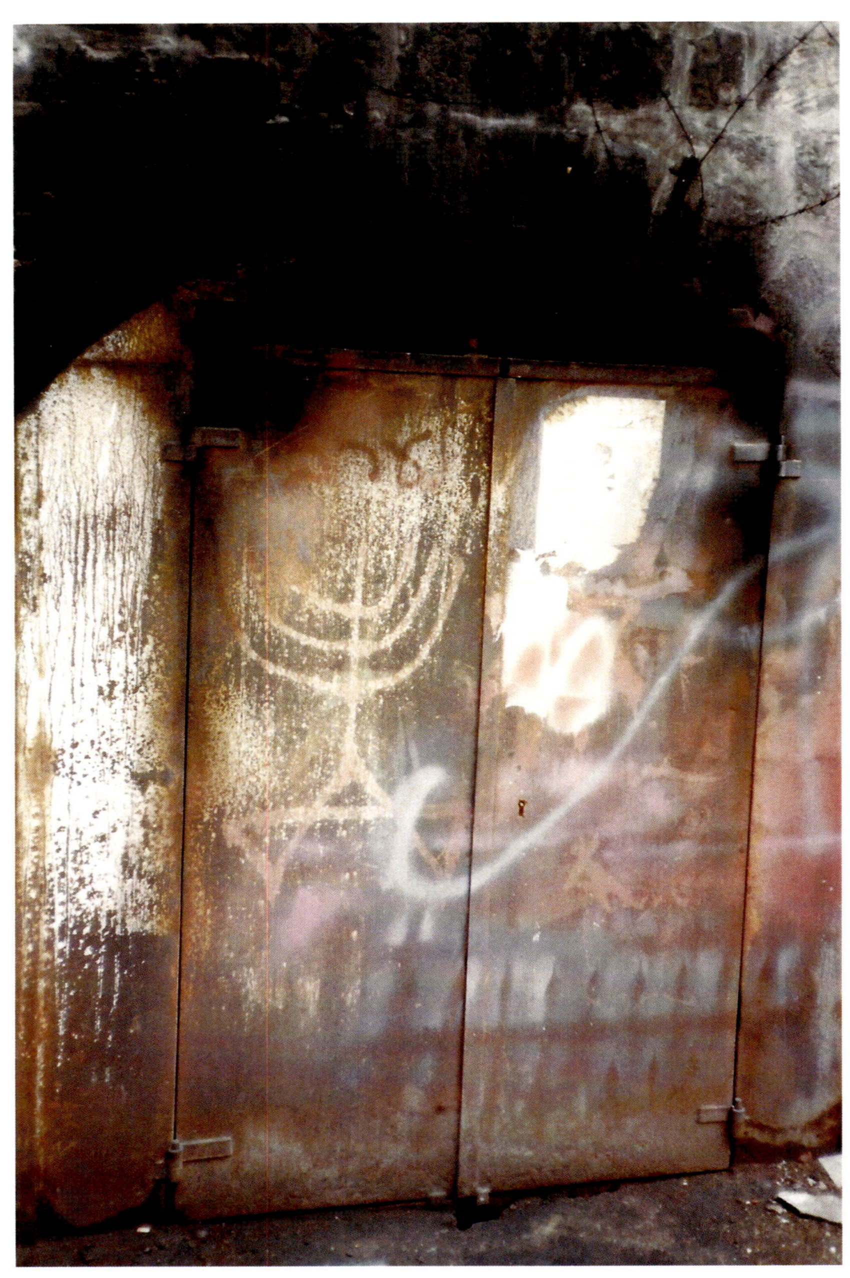

Hebron 2000

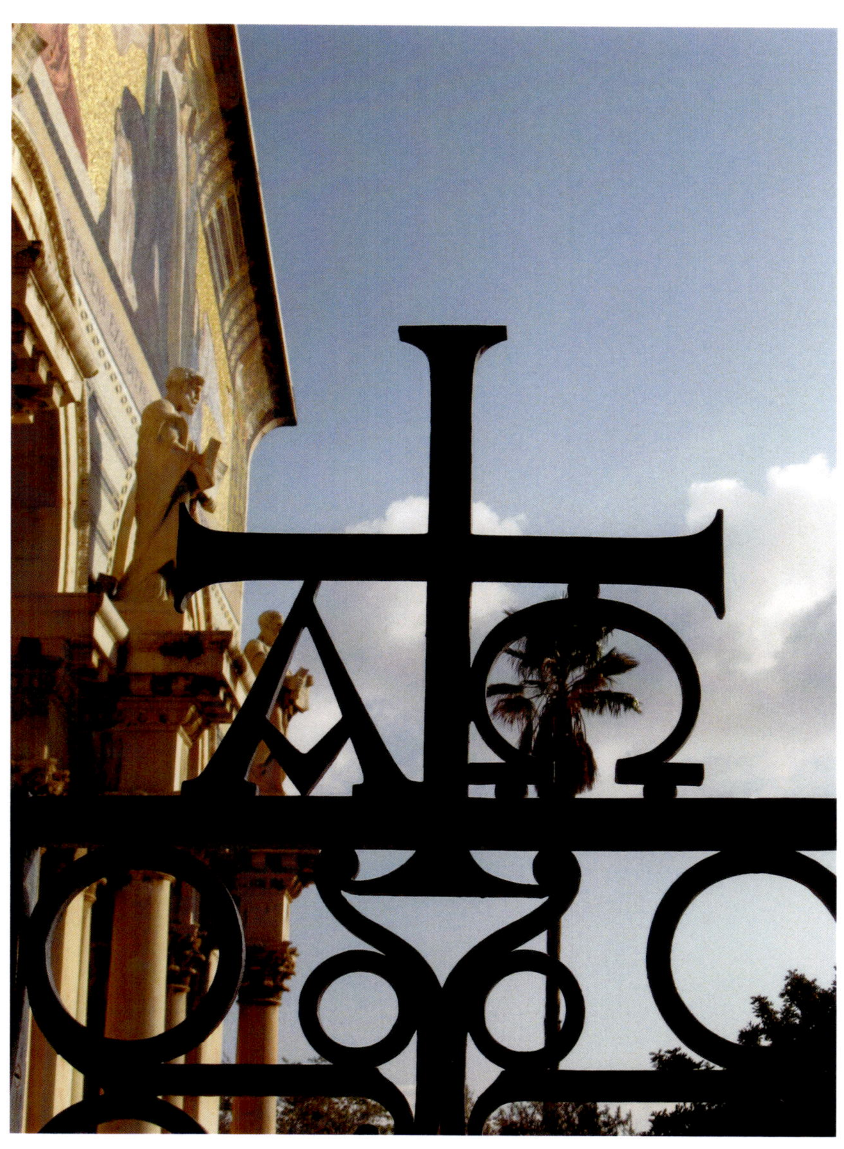

Garden of Gethsemane 2008

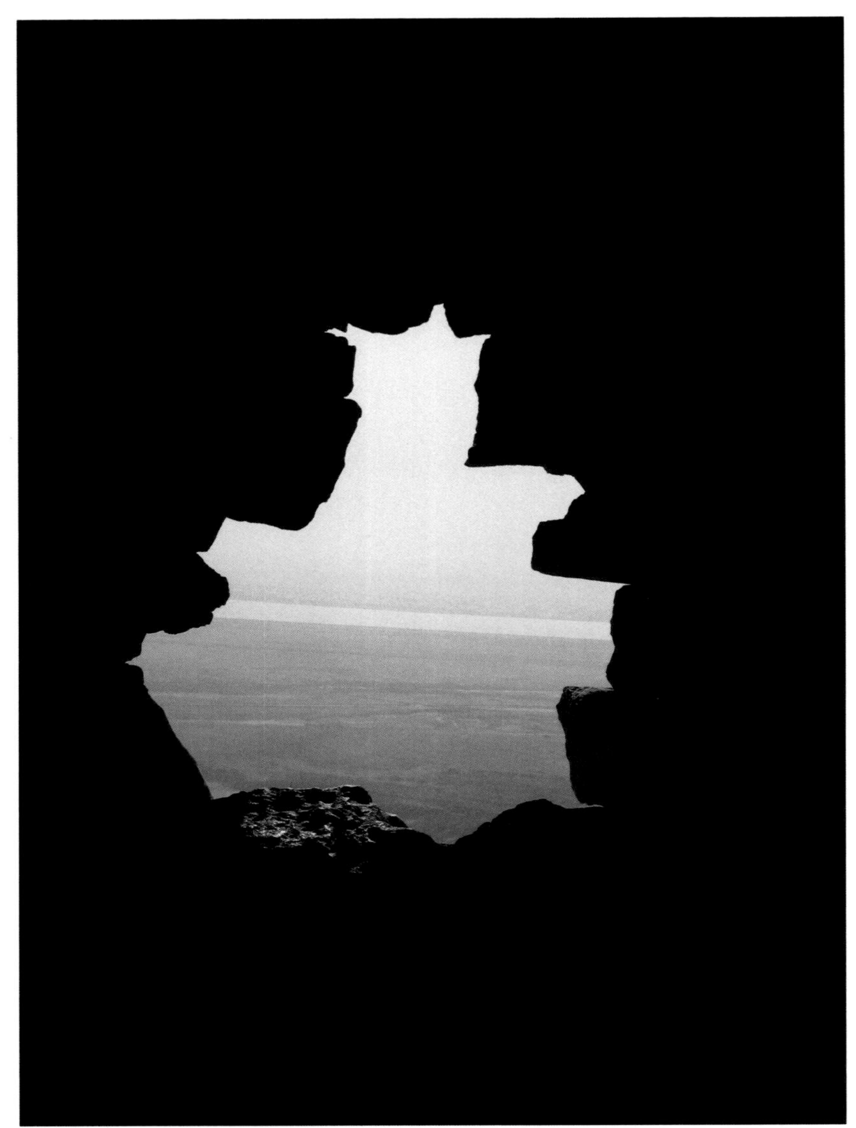

Masada 2008

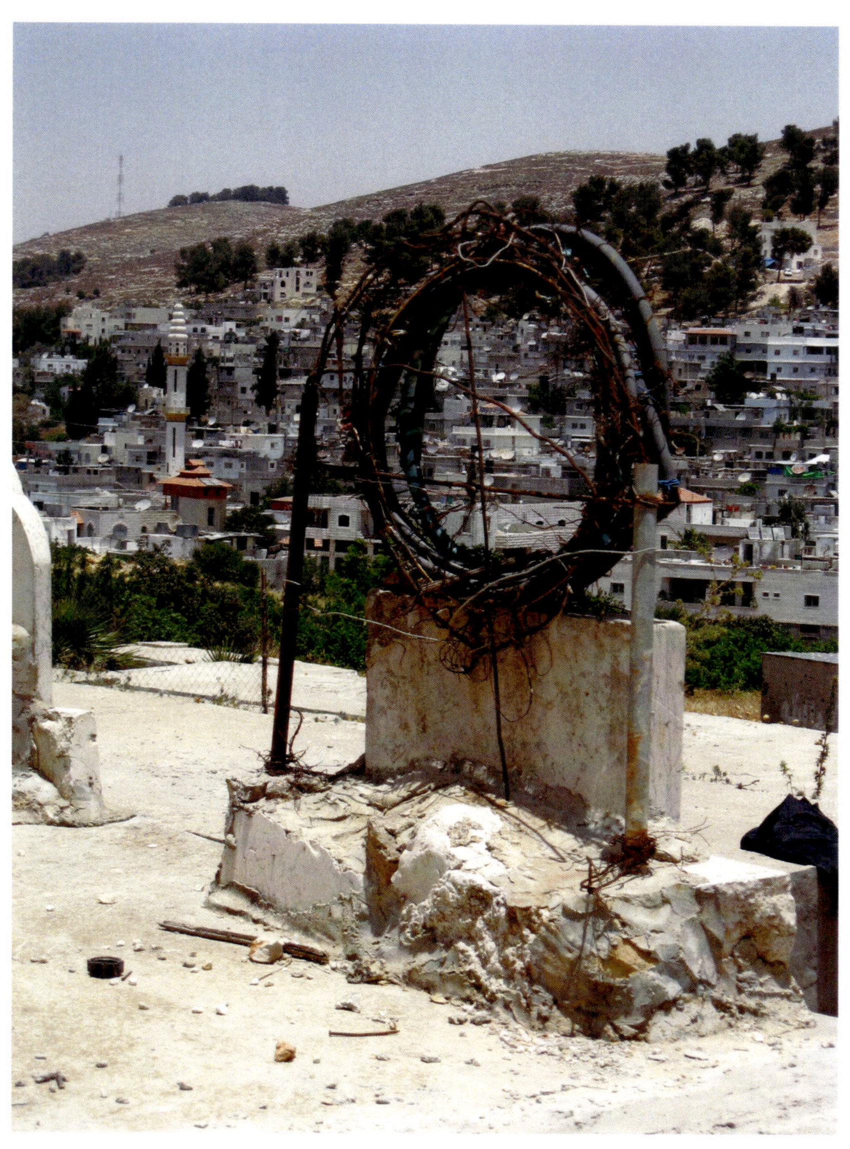

El Arroub 2010

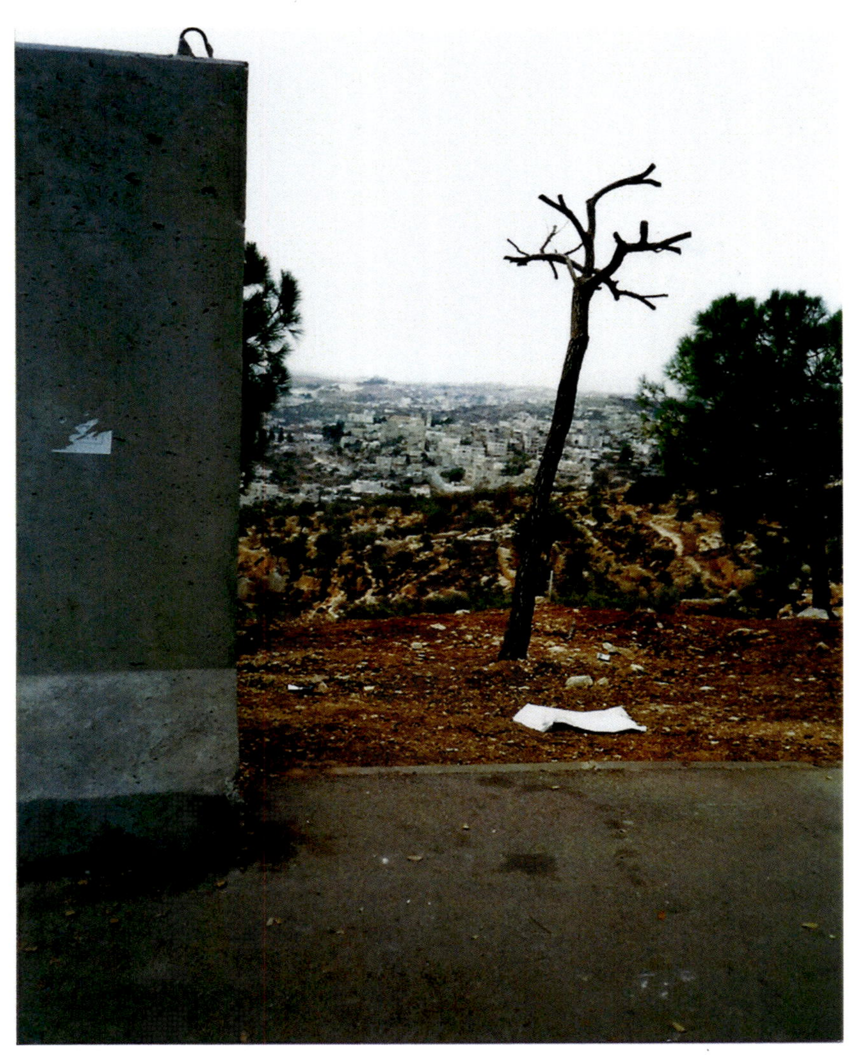

Gilo 2000

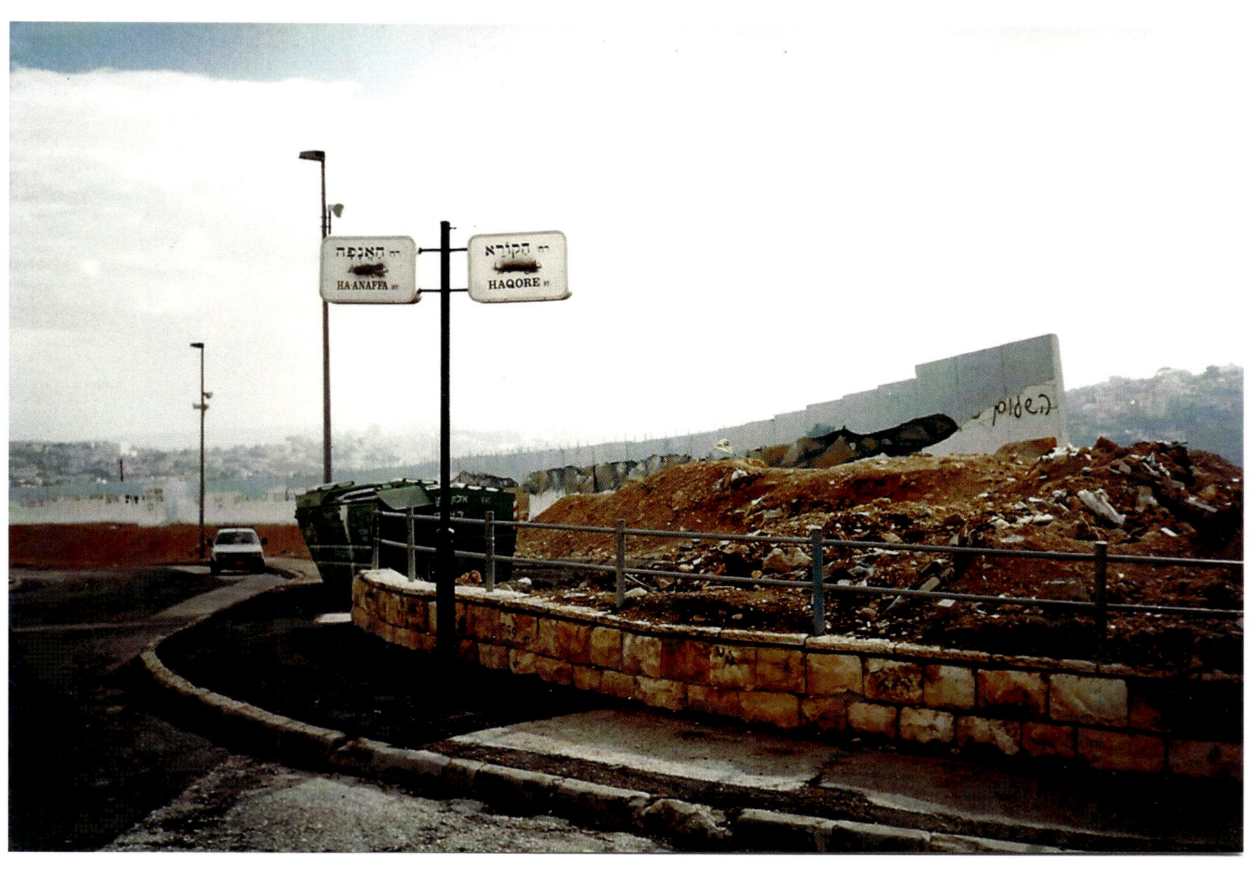

Gilo 2000

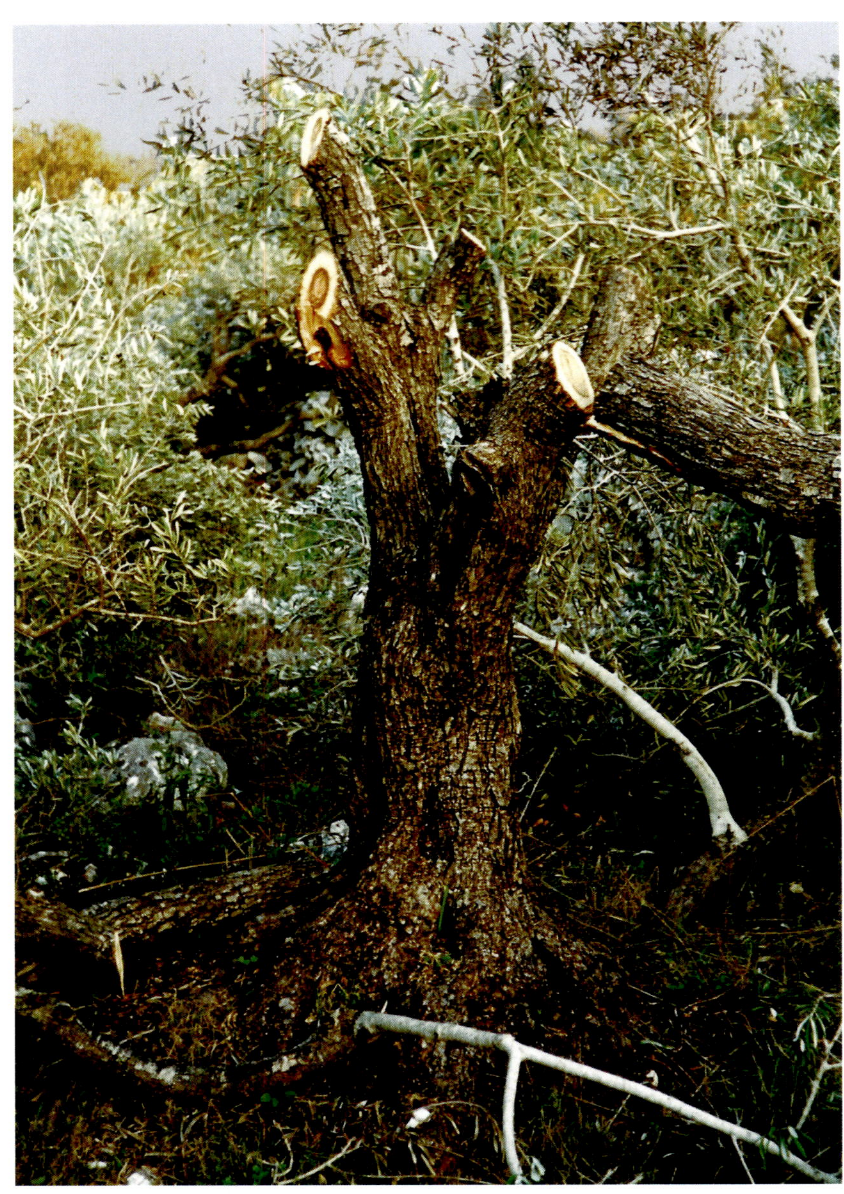

West Bank 2000

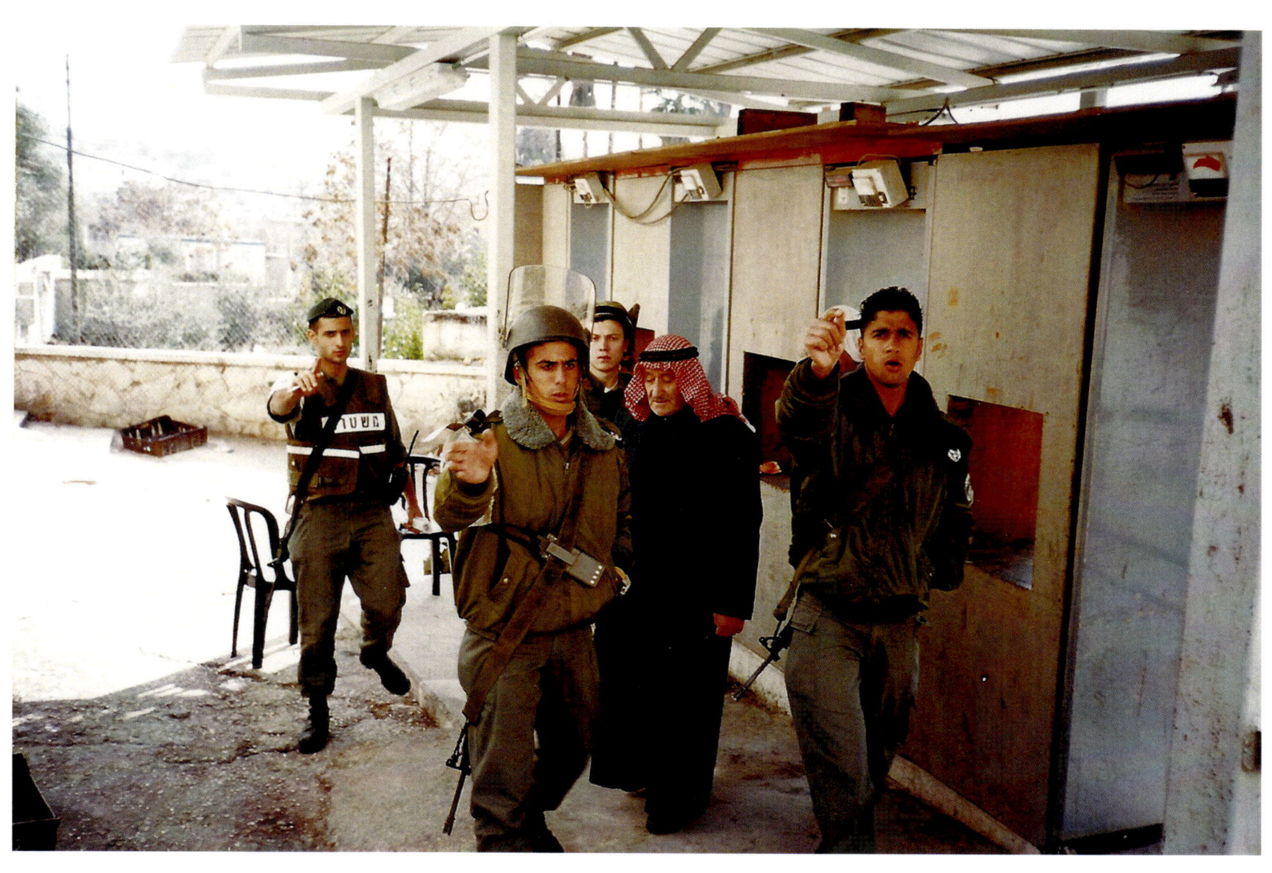

Hebron 2000

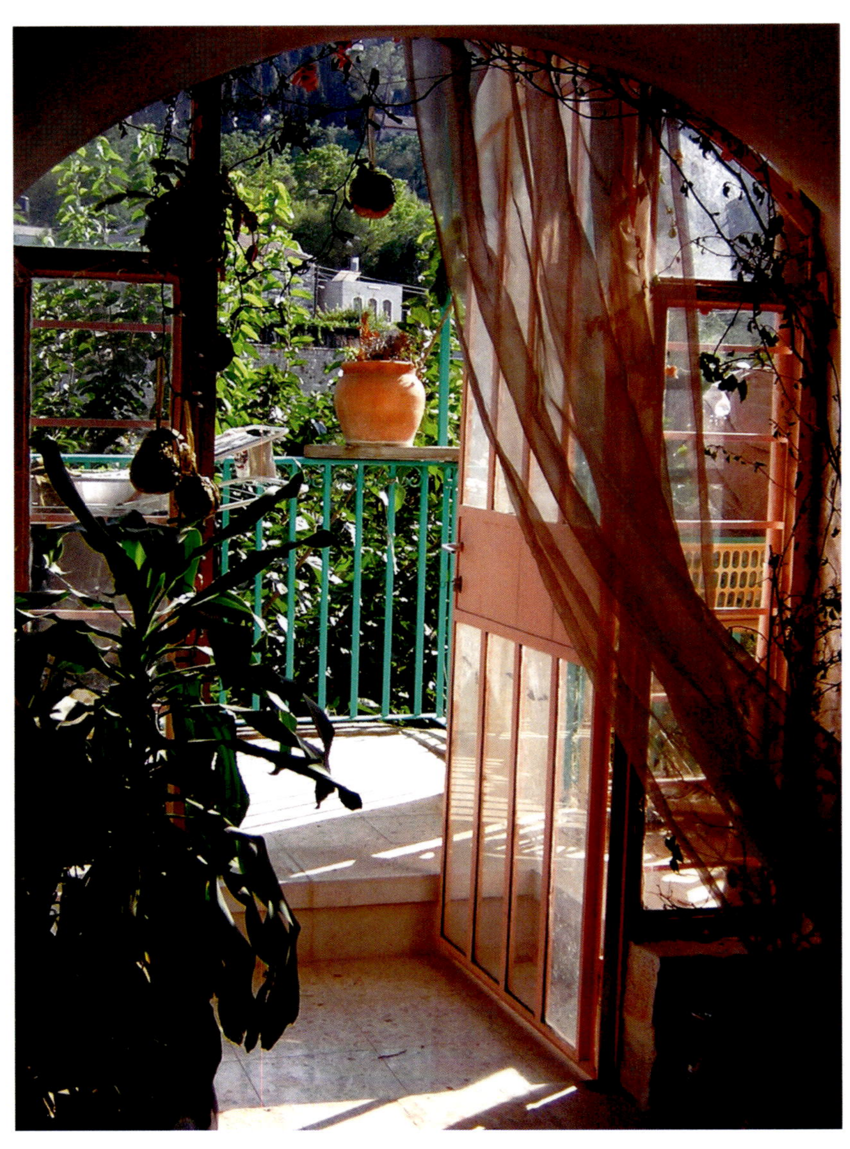

Ein Kerem 2005

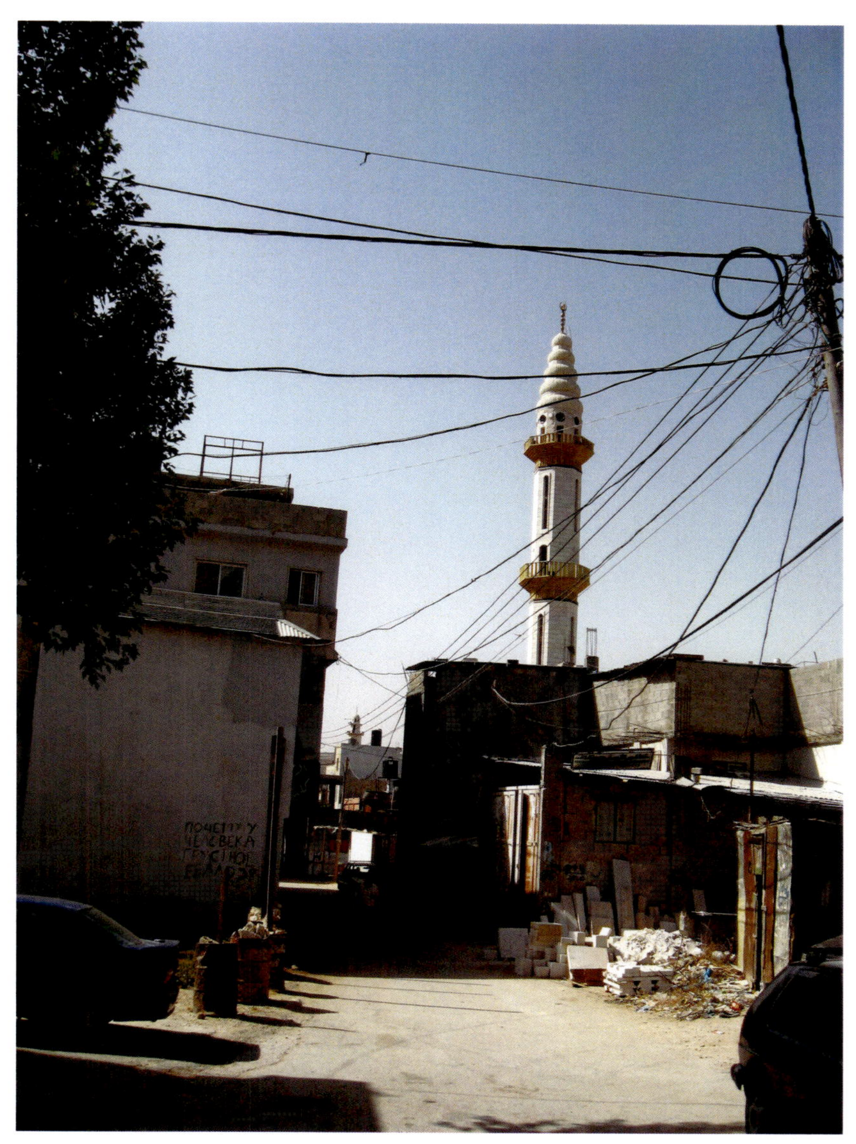

El Arroub 2010

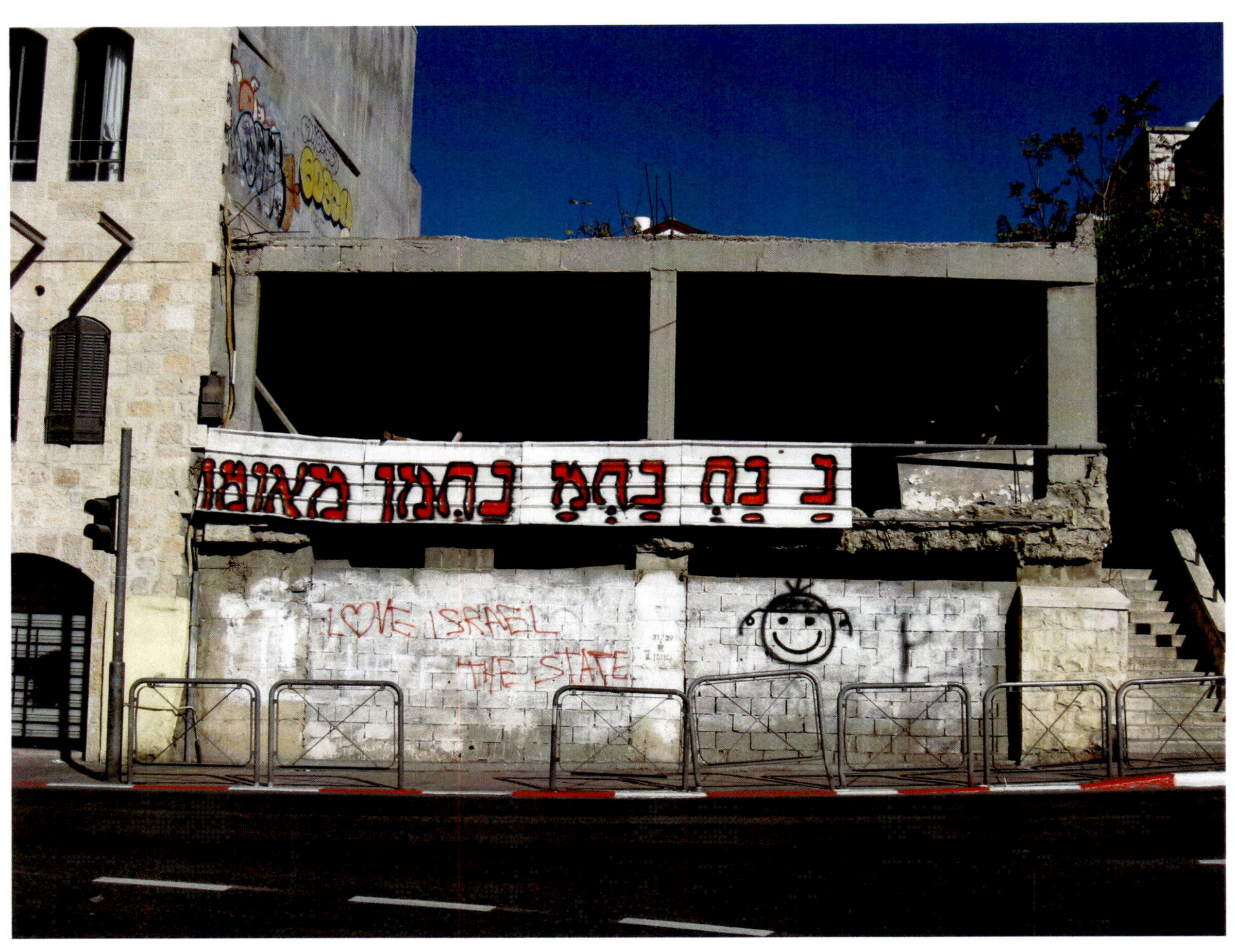

Jerusalem 2010

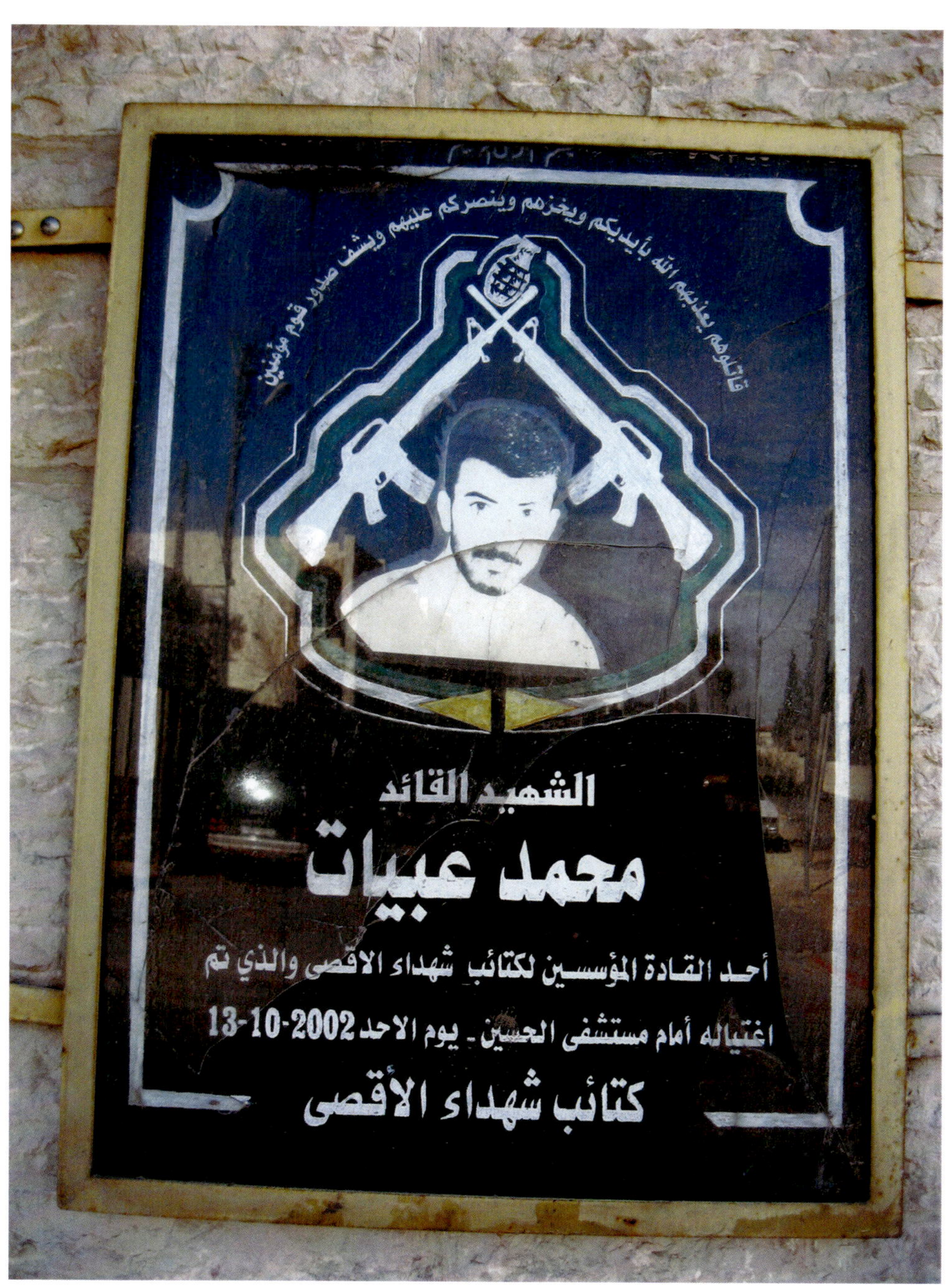

Bethlehem 2010

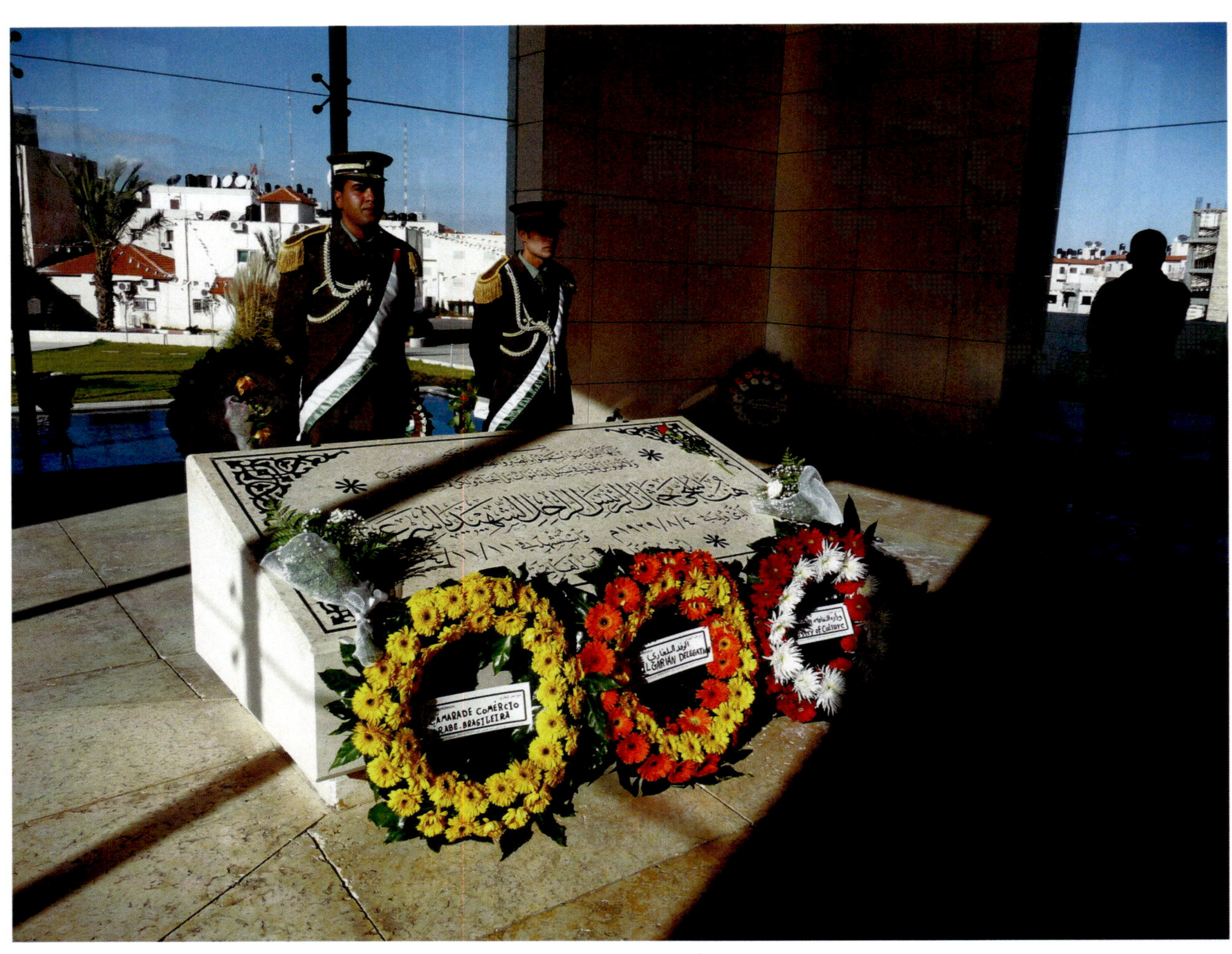

Ramallah 2010

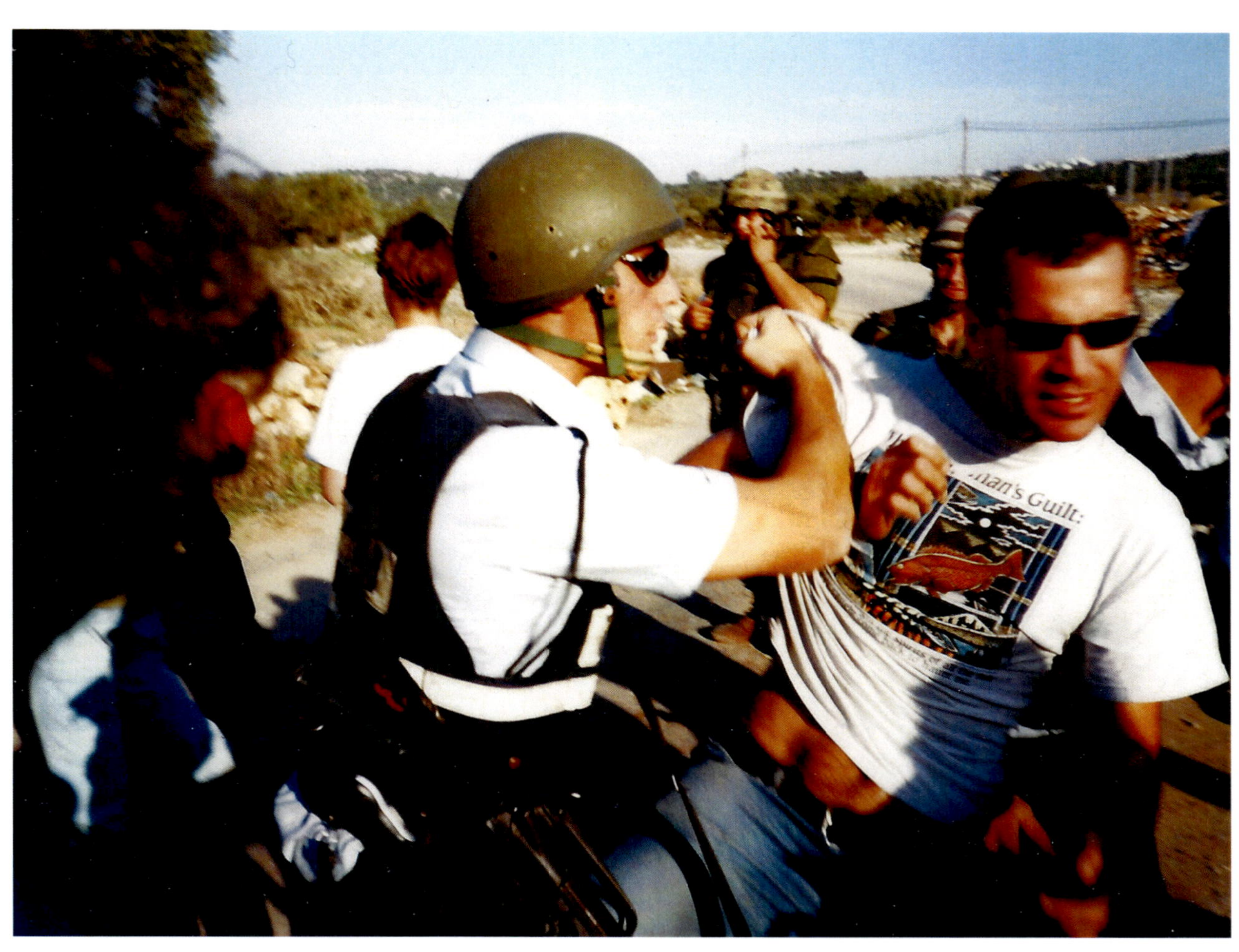

West Bank 2000

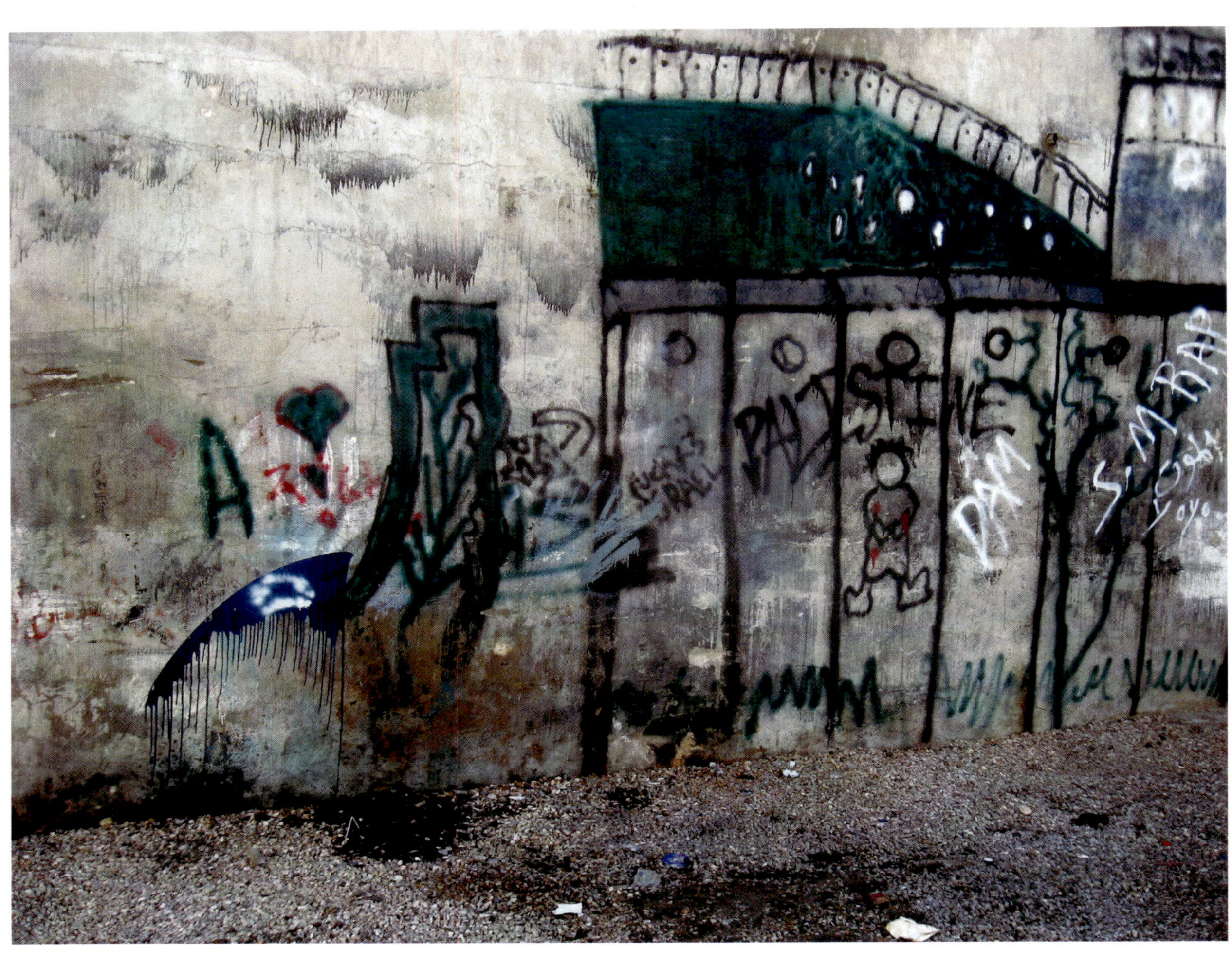

El Arroub 2010

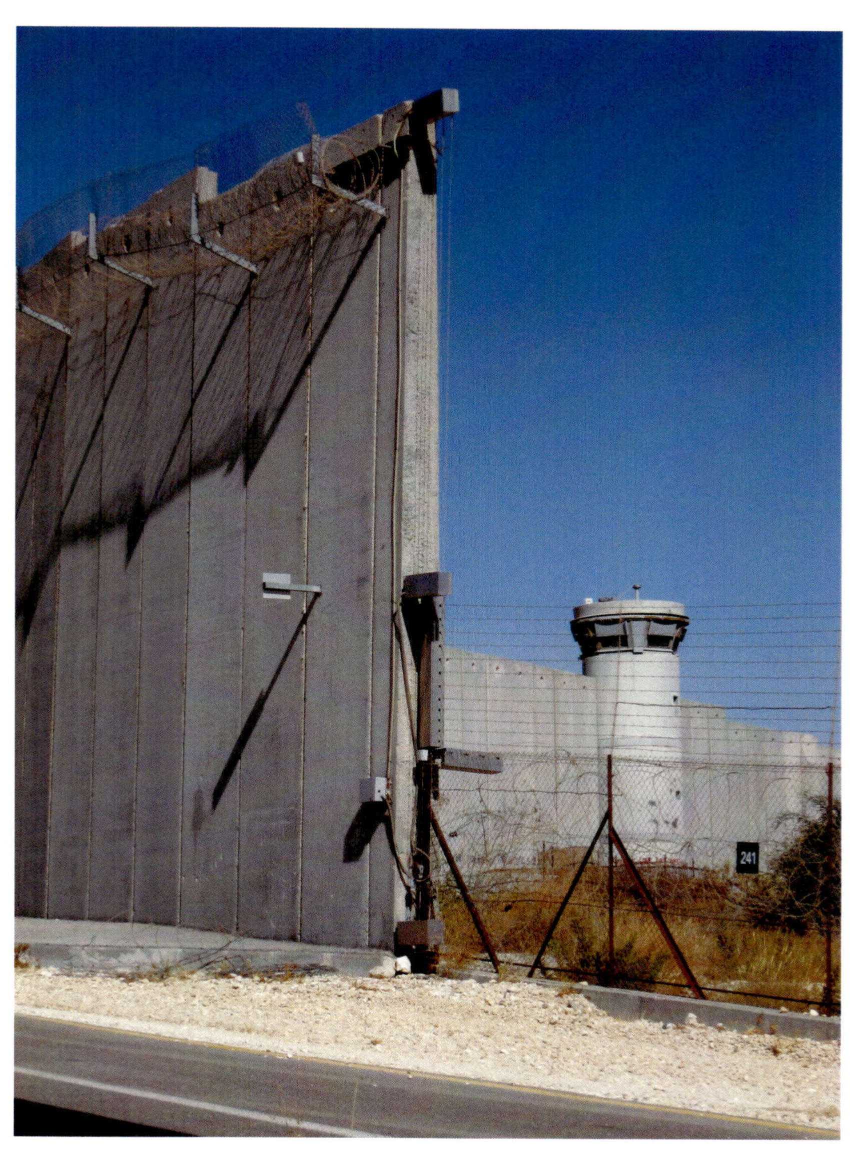

Separation Wall 2010

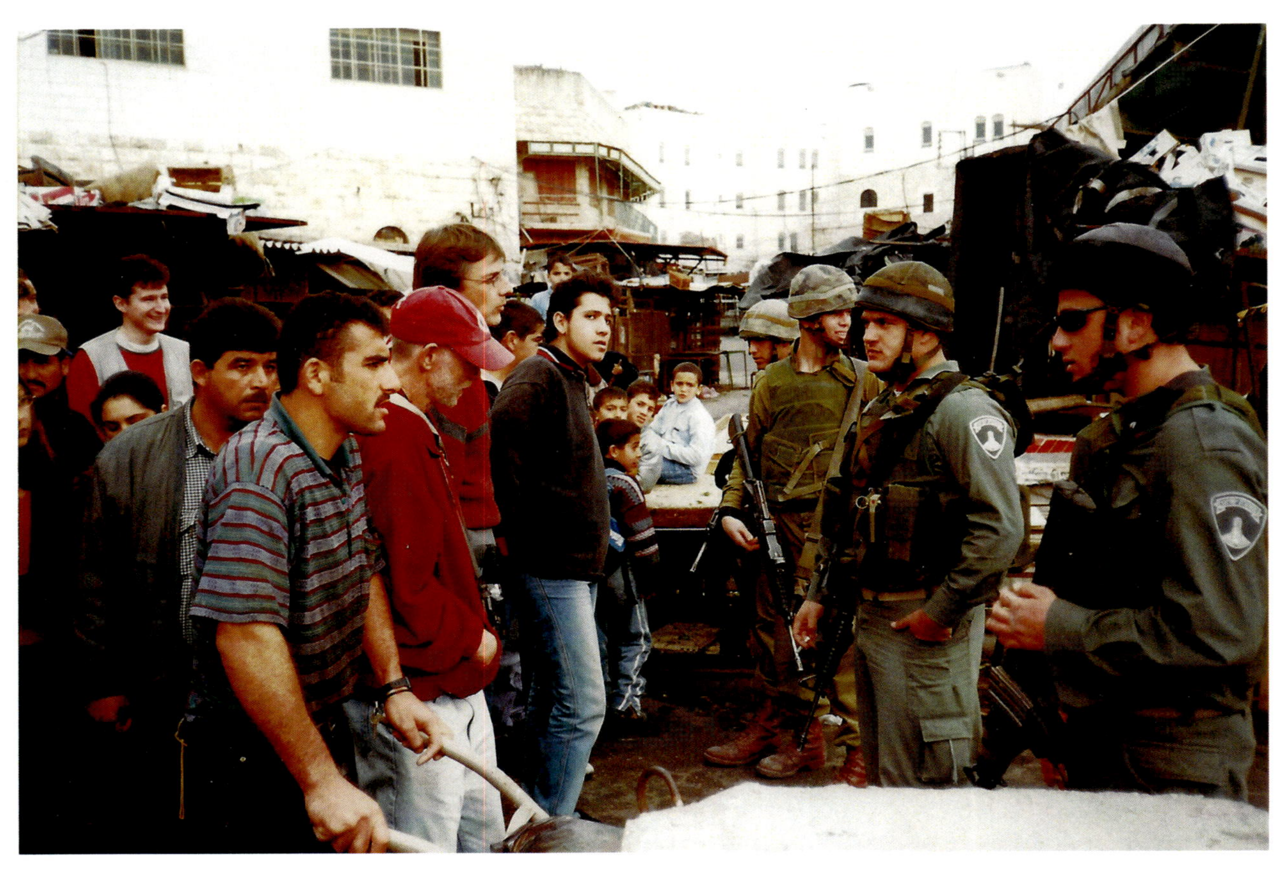

Hebron 2000

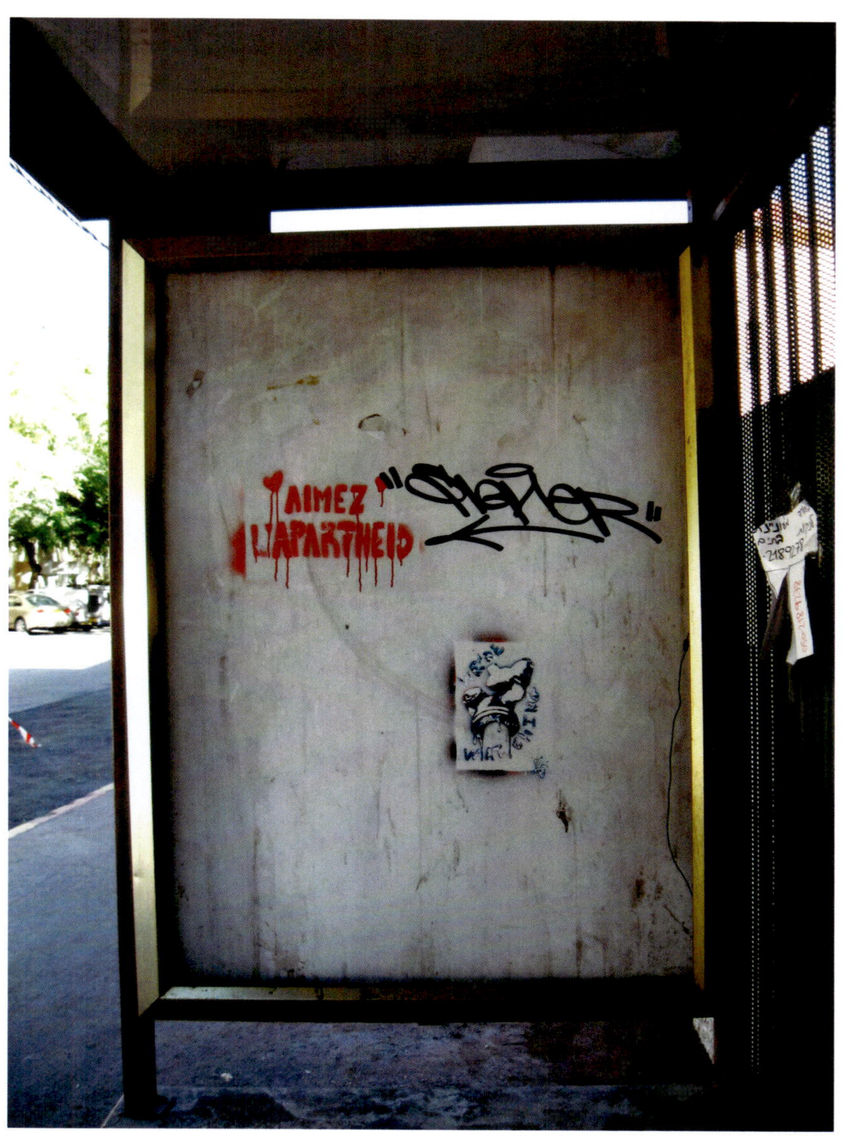

Jerusalem 2010

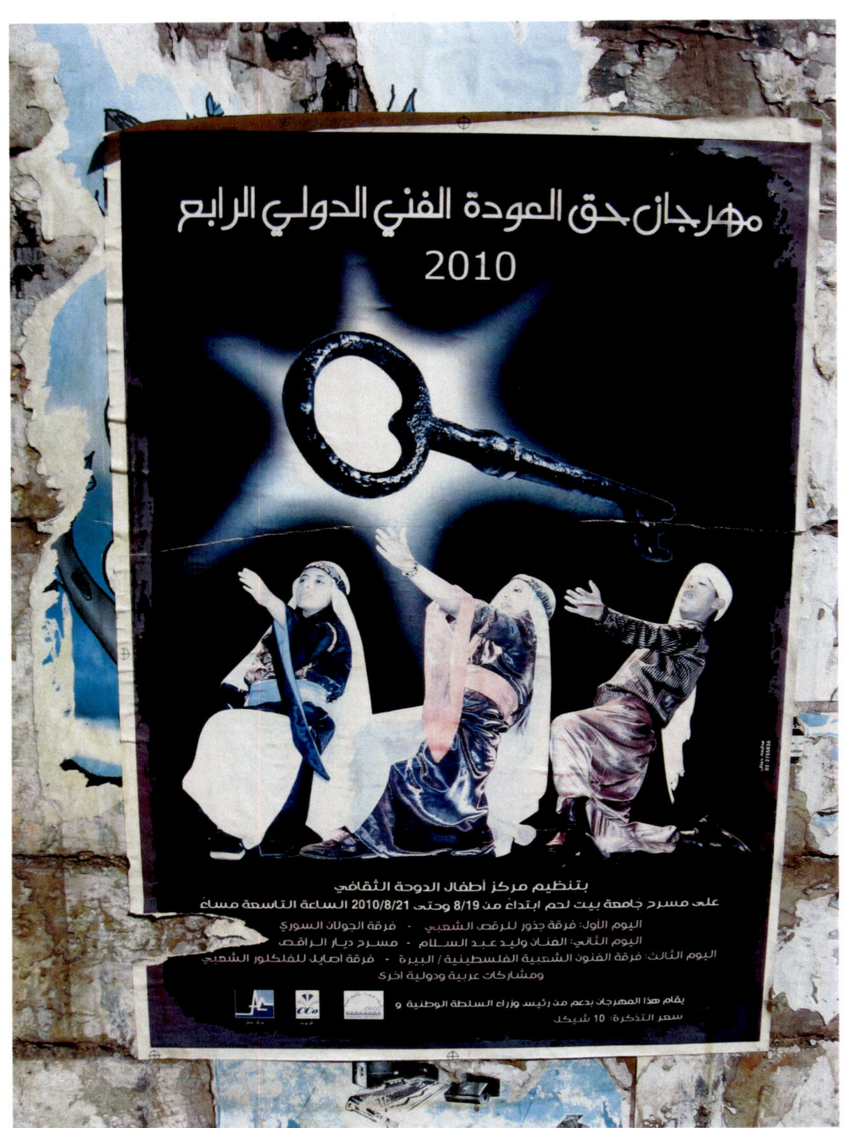

Bethlehem 2010

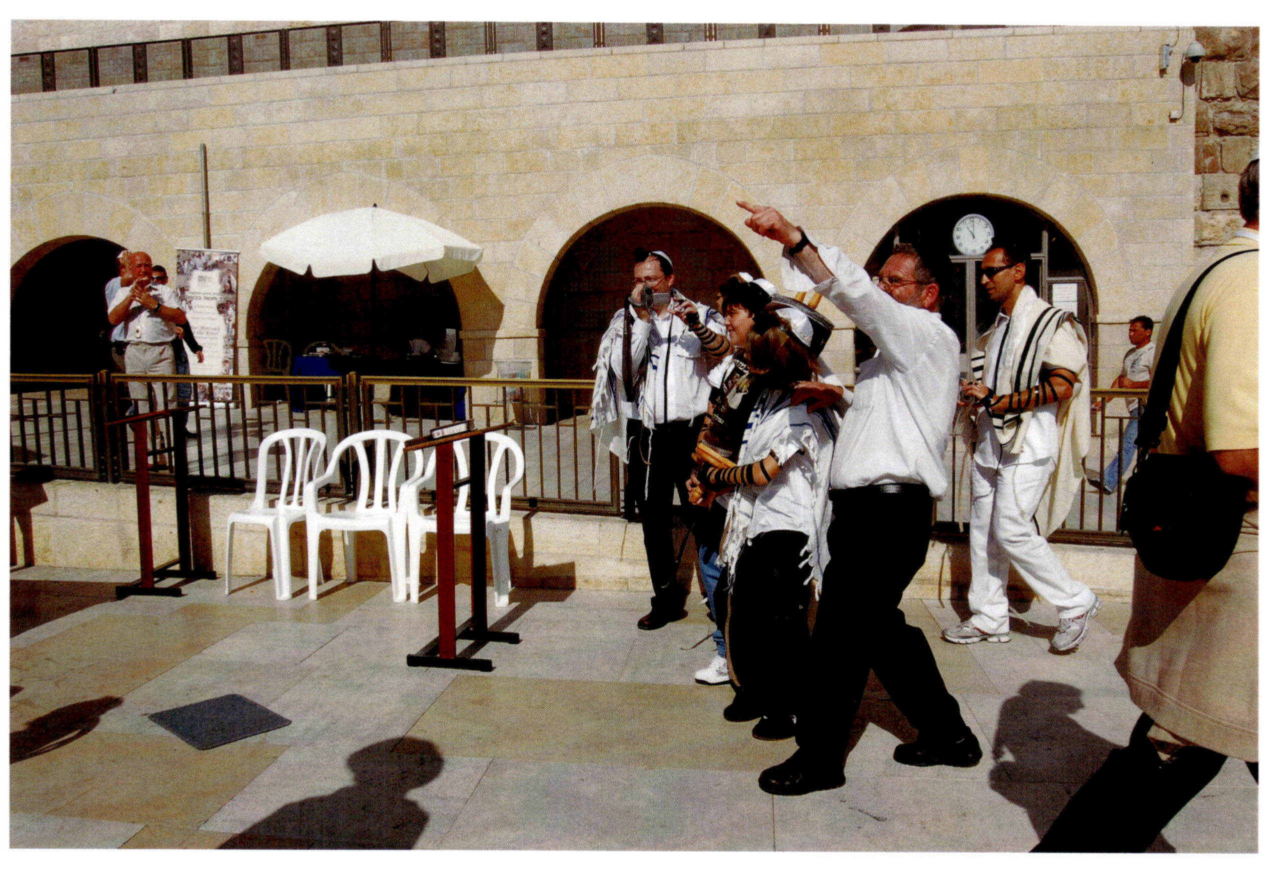

Old City, Jerusalem 2009

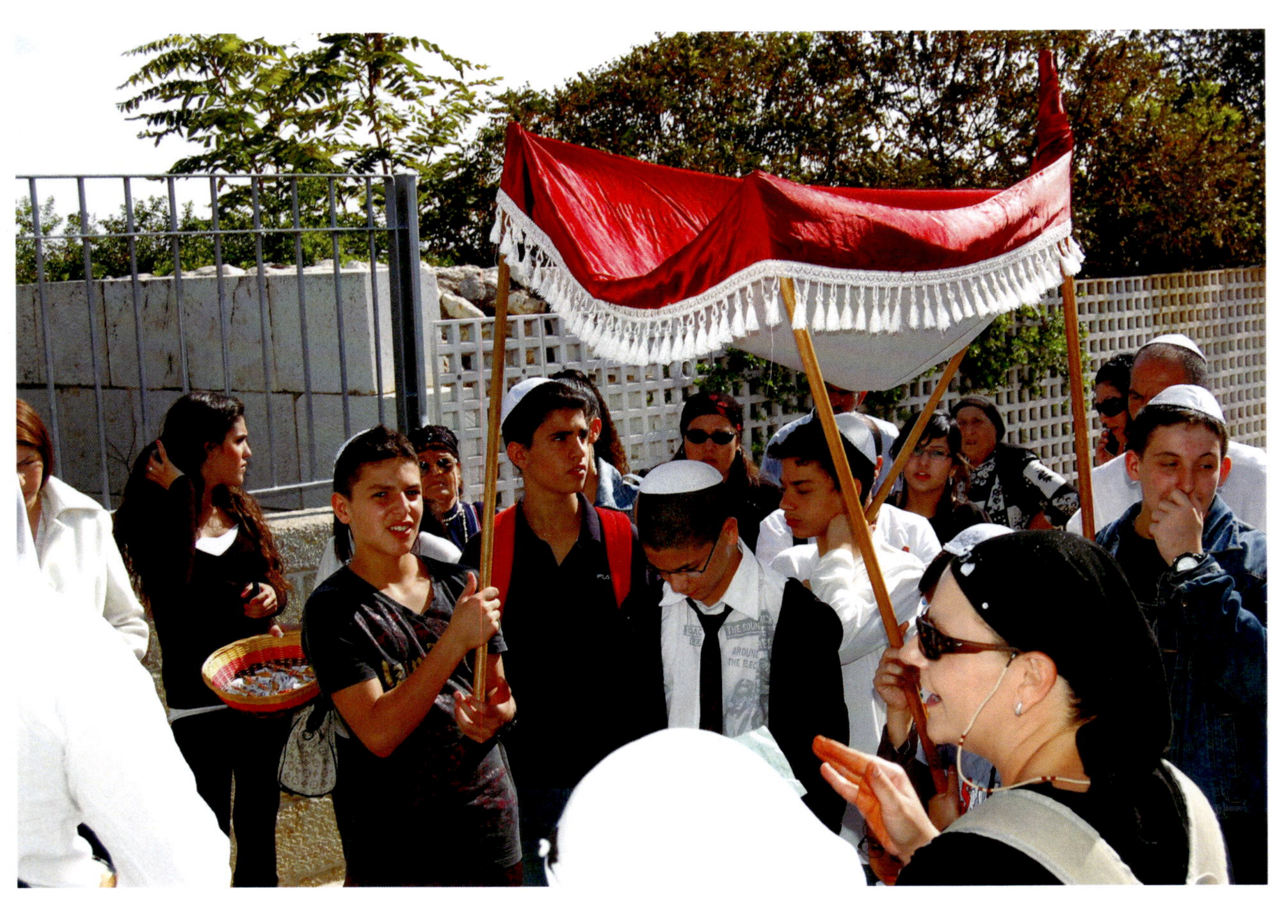

Old City, Jerusalem 2009

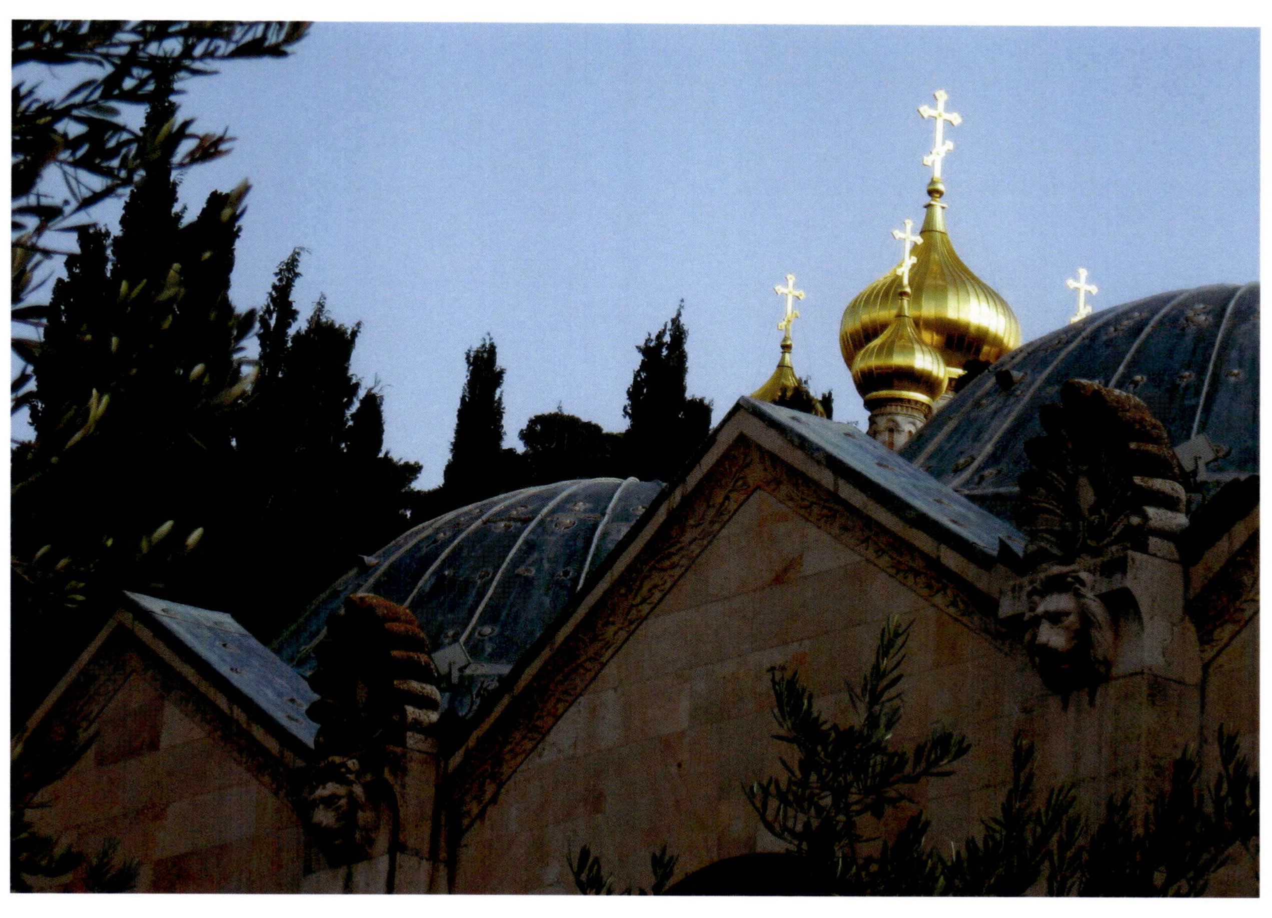

Garden of Gethsemane 2008

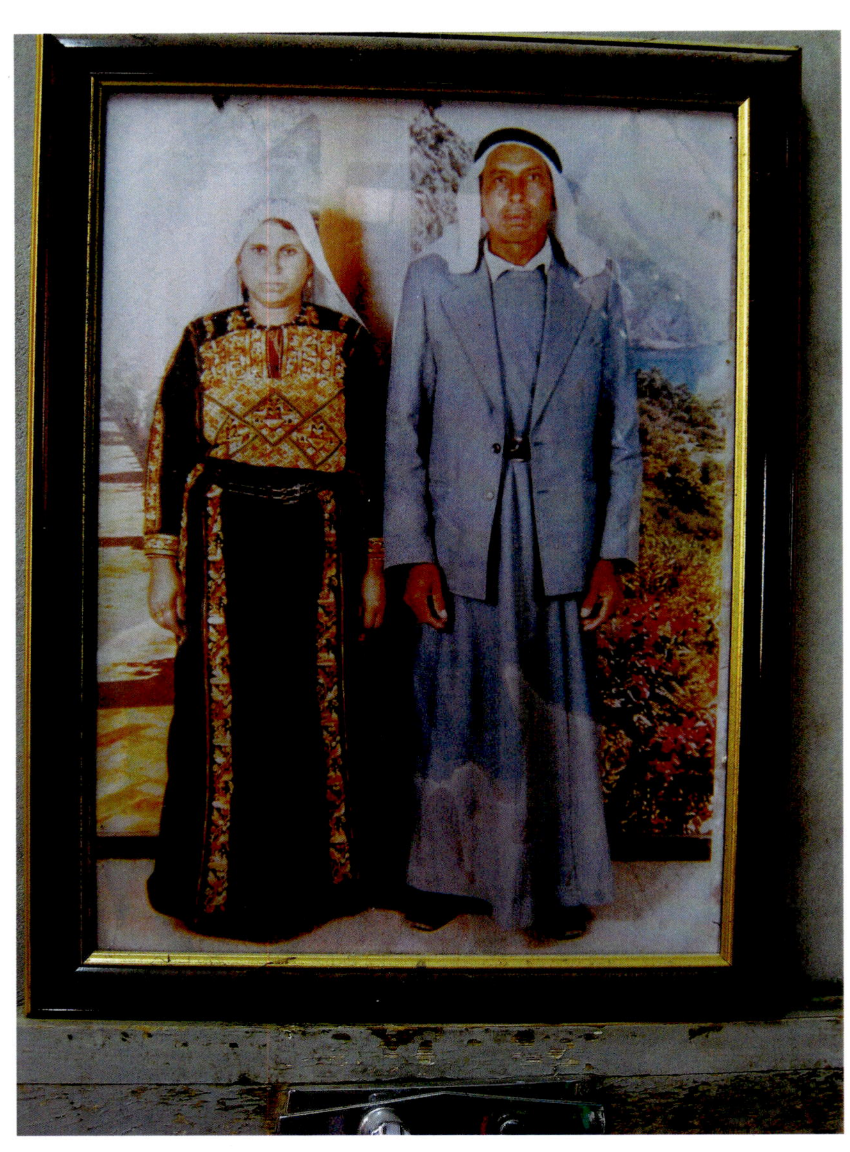

El Arroub 2010

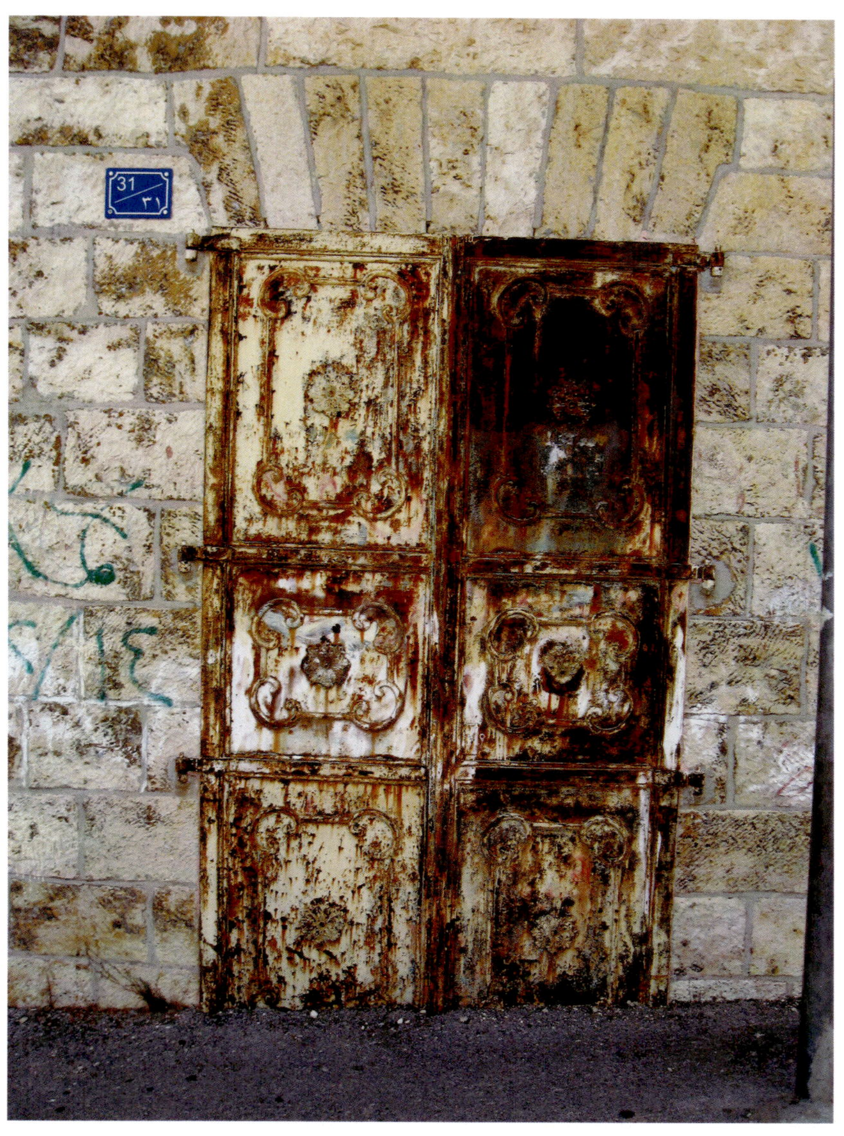

Bethlehem 2010

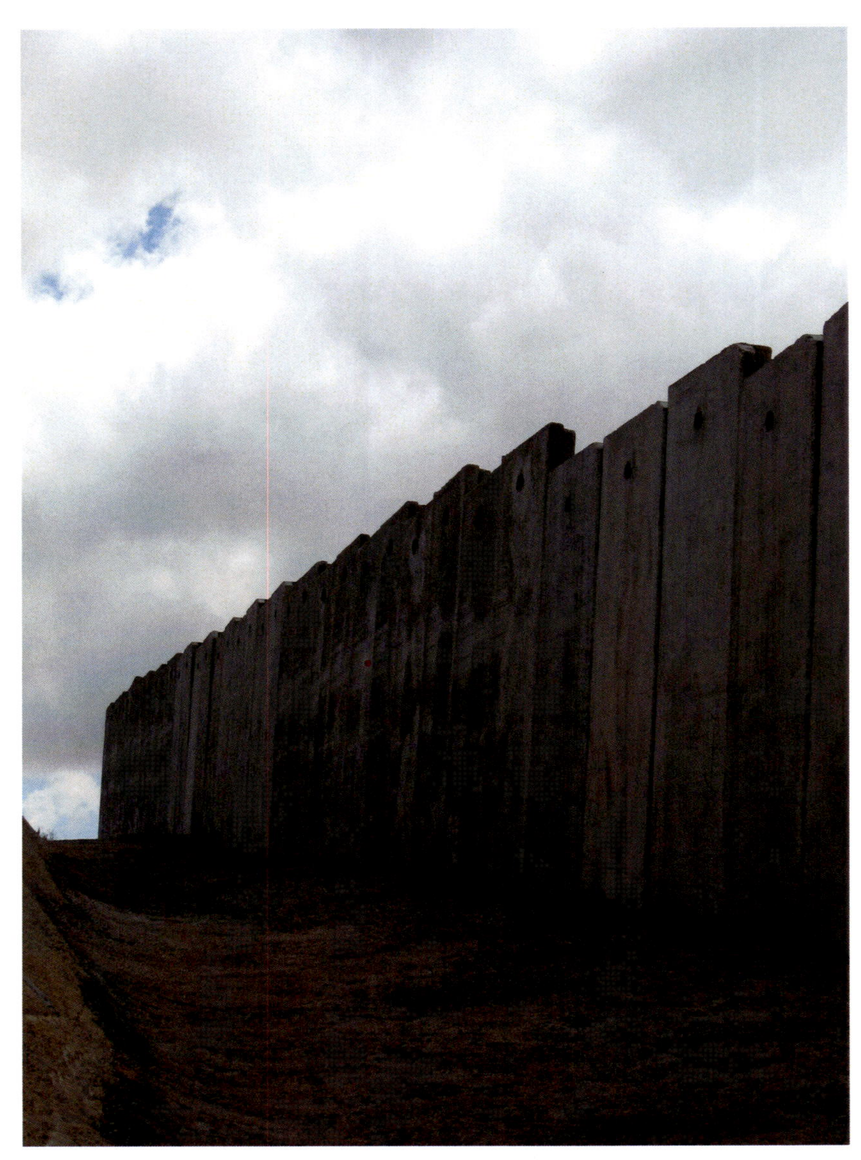

Separation Wall 2010

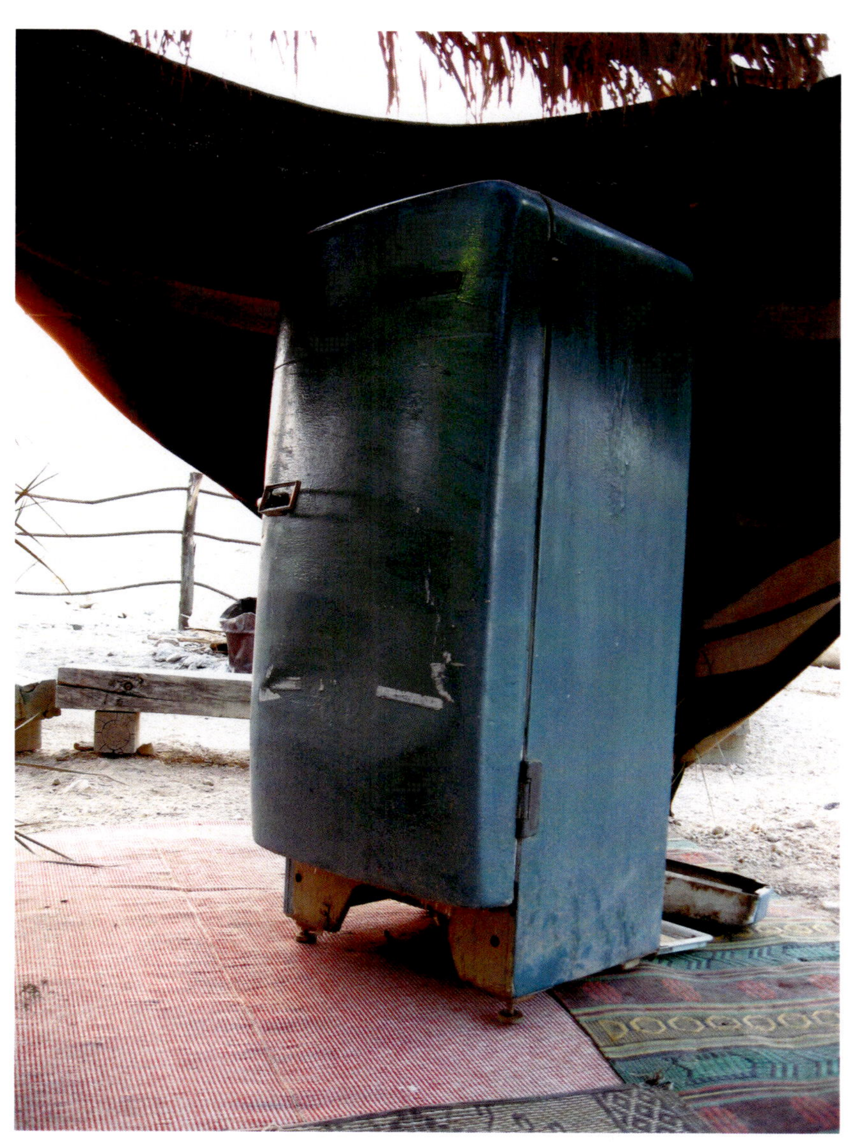

Negev Desert 2007

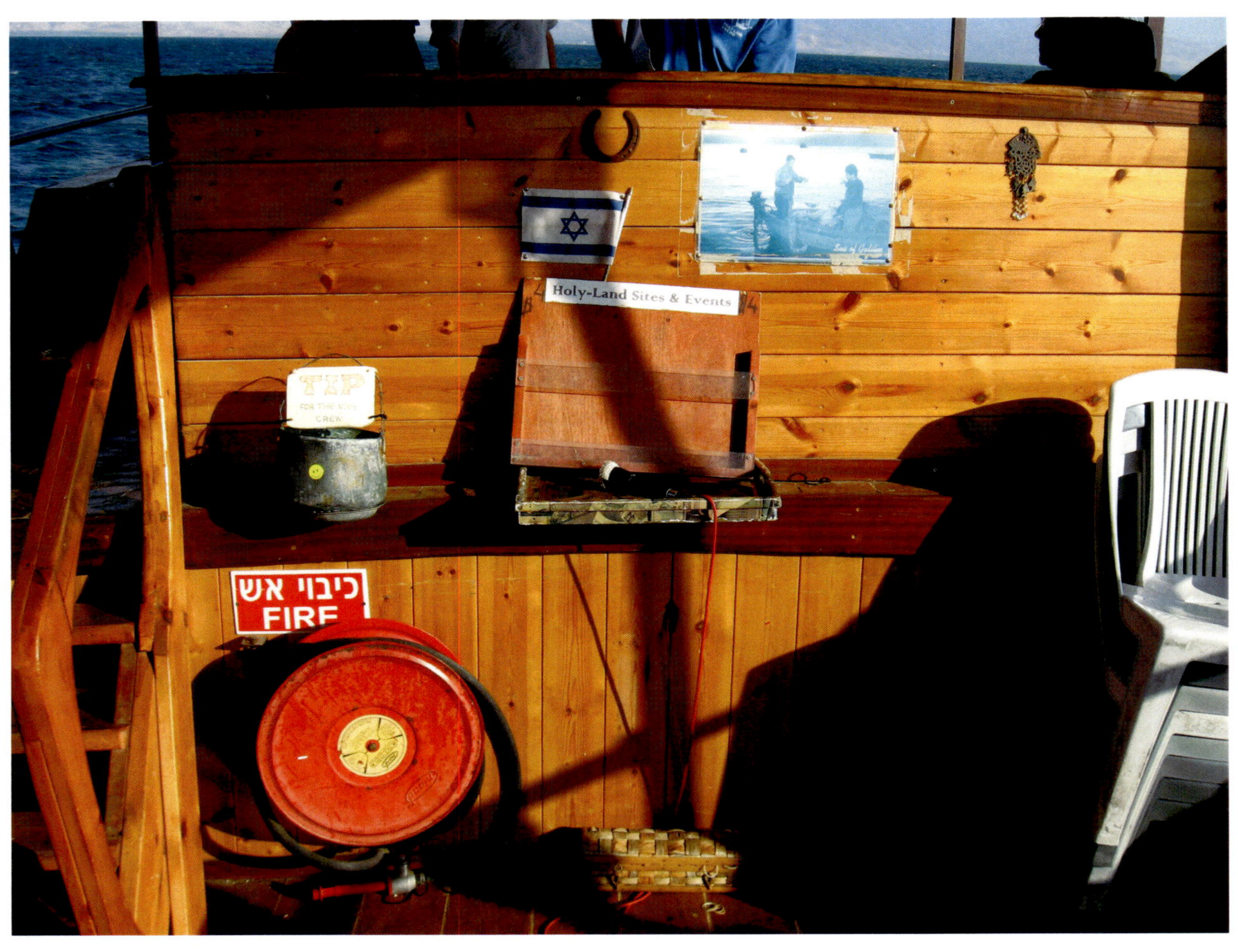

Sea of Galilee 2007

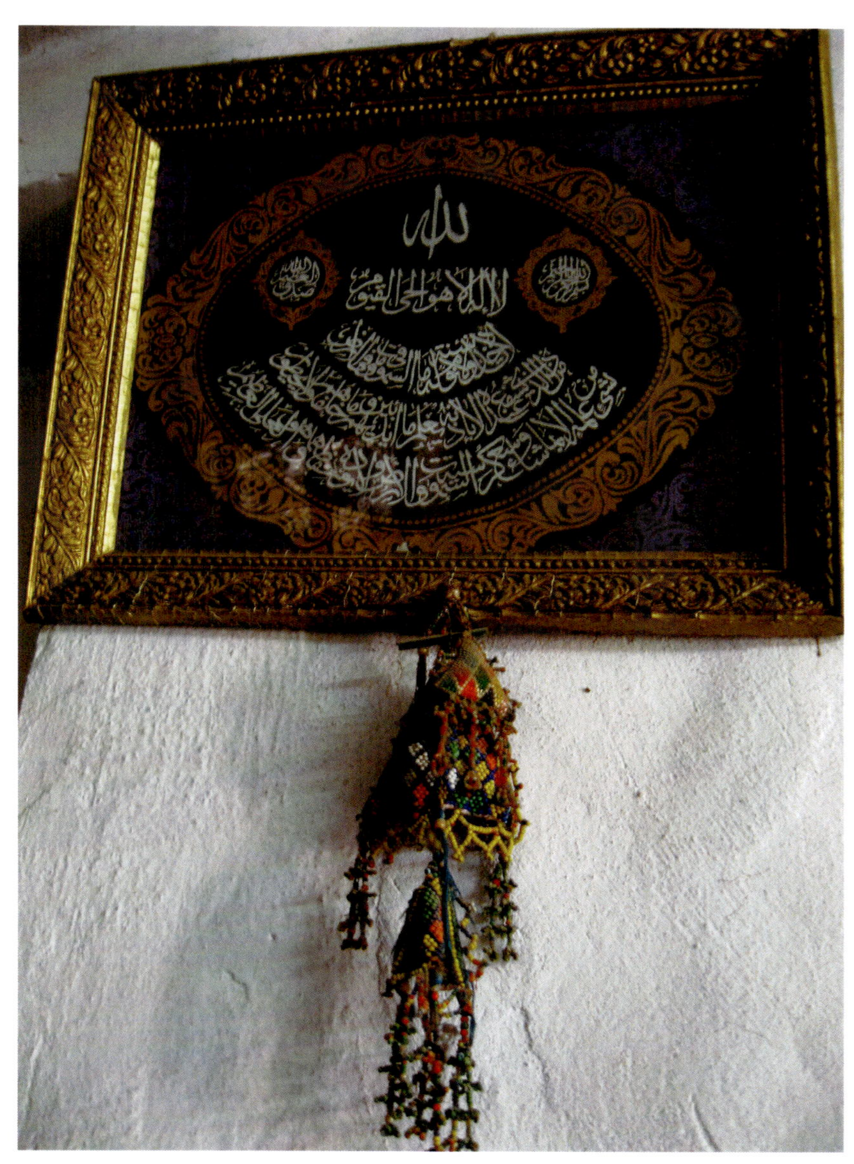

El Arroub 2010

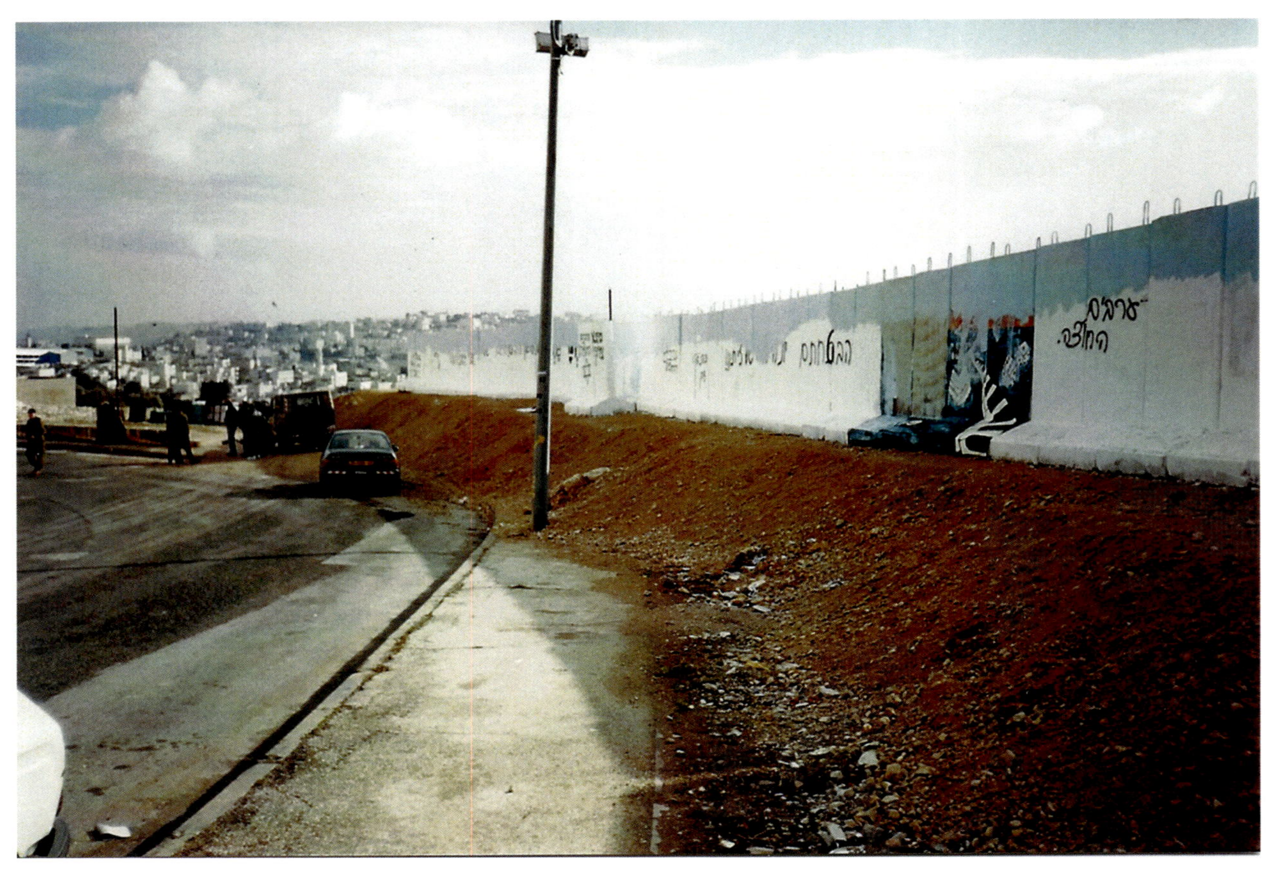

Gilo 2000

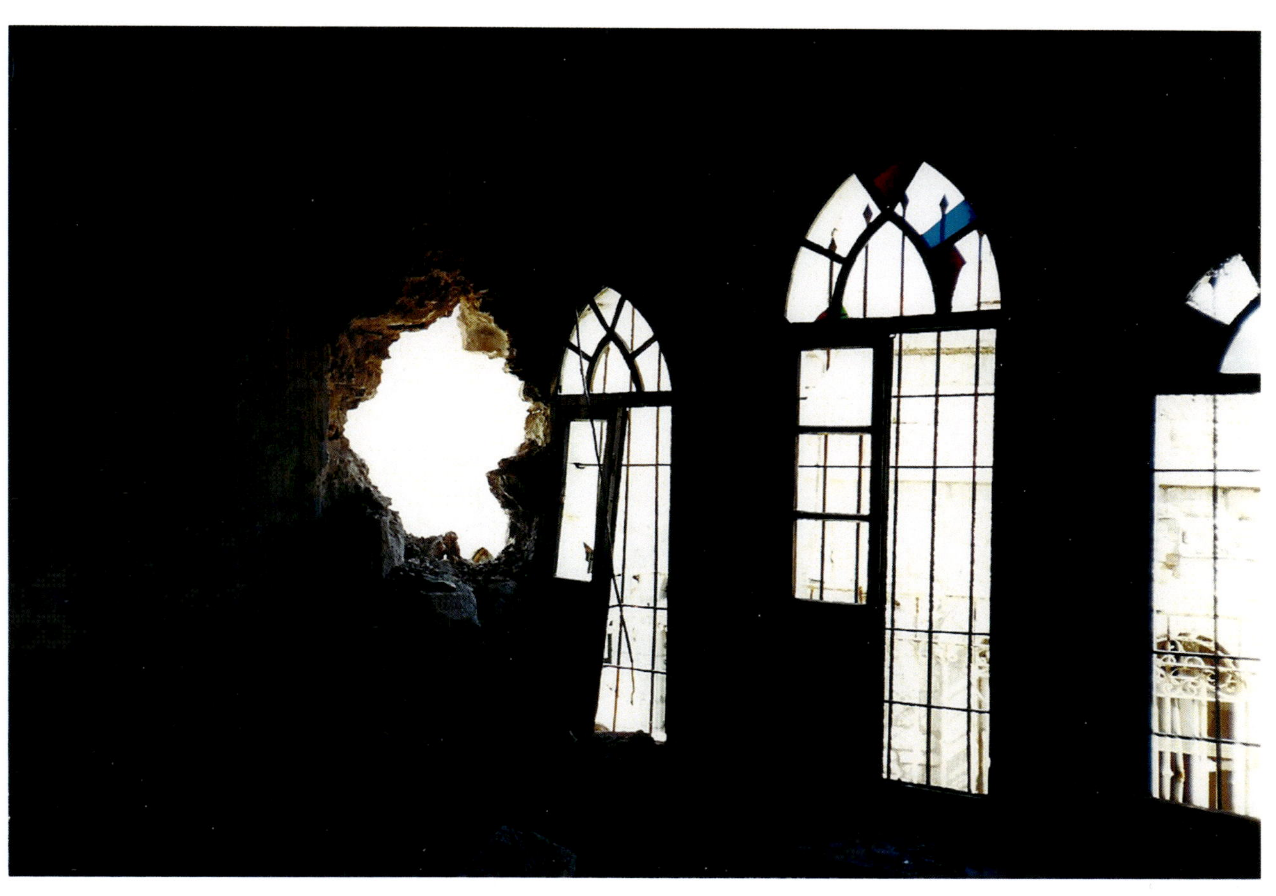

Beit Jala 2000

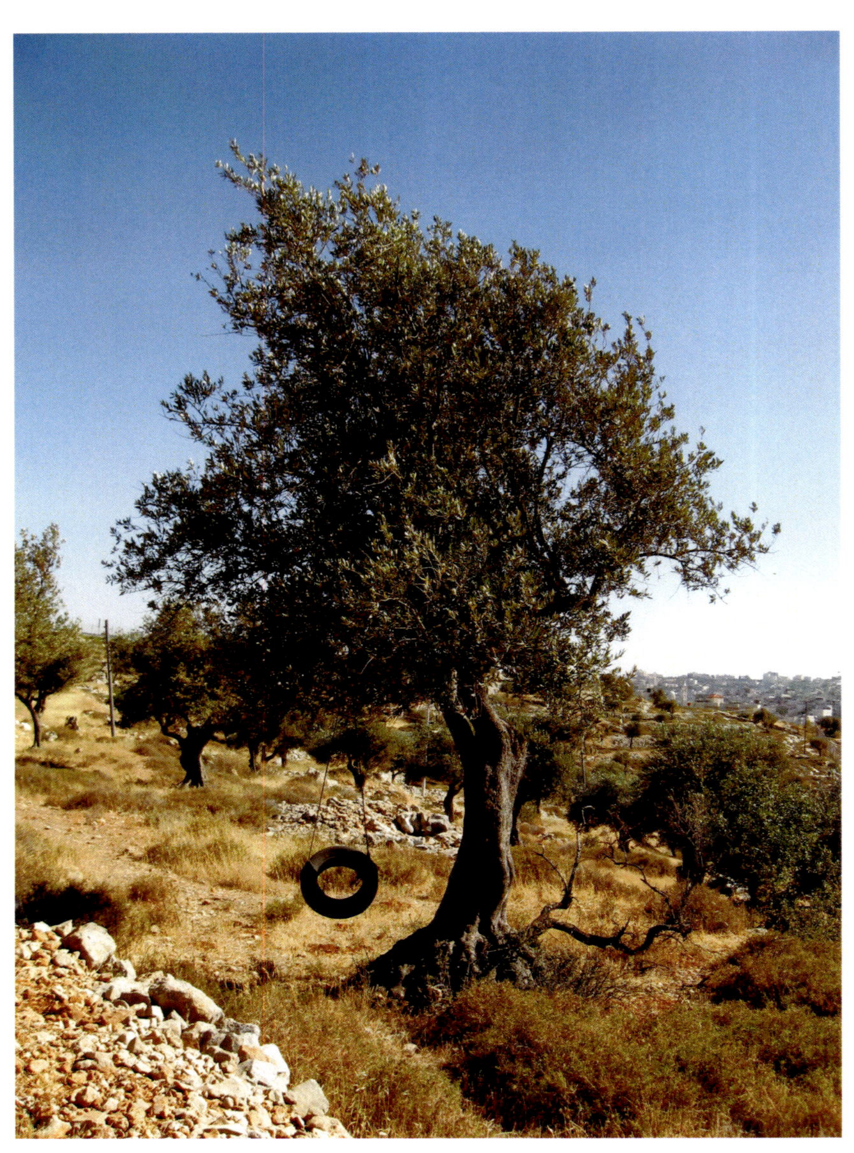

Green Line 2010

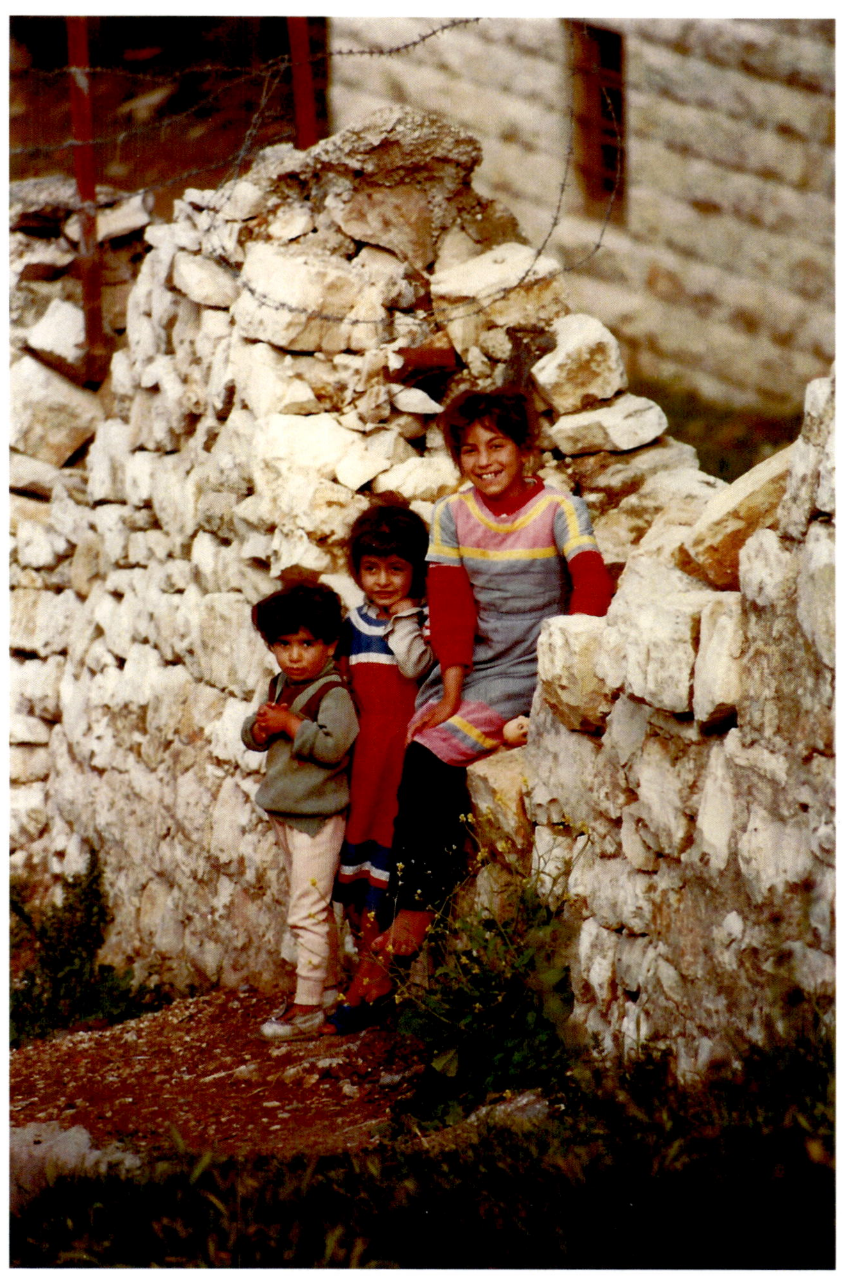

El Arroub 1988